WINNING THE
TALENT WAR

Ensuring Effective

Leadership in Healthcare

WINNING THE
TALENT WAR

Ensuring Effective
Leadership in Healthcare

Carson F. Dye

Health Administration Press
ACHE Management Series

Your board, staff, or clients may also benefit from this book's insight. For more information on quantity discount, contact the Health Administration Press Marketing Manager at (312) 424-9470.

06   05   04   03   02   5   4   3   2   1

Library of Congress Cataloging-in-Publication Data

Dye, Carson F.
    Winning the talent war : ensuring effective leadership in healthcare /
    by Carson F. Dye.
        p. cm.
    Includes bibliographical references and index.
    ISBN 1-56793-179-0
        1. Health services administration.   2. Leadership.   I. Title.

    RA971 .D944 2002
    362. 1'068'4—dc21   2002020153

The paper used in this publication meets the minimum requirements of American National Standard for Information Sciences—Permanence of Paper for Printed Library Materials, ANSI z39.48-1984.™

Acquisitions Editor: Audrey Kaufman; Project manager: Cami Cacciatore; Cover/text design: Matt Avery

Health Administration Press
A division of the Foundation of the American College of Healthcare Executives
1 North Franklin Street, Suite 1700
Chicago, IL 60606-3491
(312) 424-2800

Table of Contents

For those who constantly
look for the exceptional in leadership and
who know this makes the greatest difference.
And to my family—
Joaquina, Carly, Emily, Liesl, and Blakely.

Foreword

IN AN INTERVIEW that was published in 1998, Warren Bennis, Ph.D., a well-known author and consultant, provides us with one of the best definitions of leadership: "A leader is one who manifests direction, integrity, hardiness, and courage in a consistent pattern of behavior that inspires trust, motivation, and responsibility on the part of followers who, in turn, become leaders themselves."

The acid test of leadership is the selection and development of other leaders within an organization. Jack Welch, the immediate past president and chief executive officer of General Electric, is reputed to be among the most effective business leaders of our time. Jack Welch has also selected and developed a large number of leaders who have gone on to become chief executive officers of major corporations in the United States. Many of the great health-care chief executive officers, like Gail Warden, president of Henry Ford Health System in Detroit, and Ted Bowen, former president and chief executive officer of The Methodist Hospital in Houston, have demonstrated their leadership by training a large number of people who have gone on to become chief executive officers and to successfully lead other organizations. The development of leaders in an organization is not just an executive function—it may be the key executive function.

Carson Dye has written a very comprehensive, readable text that outlines all aspects of selecting and developing leadership talent. This book is of value to veteran executives as well as newer executives entering the field who wish to hone their leadership talents. Moreover, he is uniquely qualified to write such a book. The very best writers are those who combine extensive, practical experience with an exhaustive amount of research. Carson Dye has a diverse background as a healthcare executive, lecturer, consultant, executive recruiter, and writer. He has worked with hundreds of healthcare institutions and hundreds of top executives for decades. His previous books, *Leadership in Healthcare: Values at the Top* and *Executive Excellence: Protocols for Healthcare Executives* have contributed significantly to the body of knowledge available to healthcare executives throughout the United States.

Lastly, he is a leader who has taken the time to research and write his observations so that those of us who are in the field and may only have an in-depth experience of working in three or four healthcare systems may benefit from his broad experience and excellence.

Terence F. Moore
President, MidMichigan Health

Preface

THE MOST PERTINENT statement about organizational success may be this: Effective leadership is the difference between mediocrity and excellence. When studying great organizations, effective leadership is always found.

The key, then, to developing great organizations is to secure extraordinary leadership. How to find, recruit, hire, empower, develop, and retain effective leaders should be "Job One" for all leaders. There simply is nothing more important than this.

This challenge is now compounded by a new phenomenon—a shortage of leadership talent. As John Lloyd with Witt Kieffer has said, "Where have all the leaders gone?" Demographic facts predict that the next decade will be full of new challenges as organizations try to find and retain strong leadership.

This book is built around two primary themes. First, a shortage of leadership talent exists and that shortage is worsening—not just in other industries, but in healthcare as well. Second, the quest to find and keep that great talent should be the top strategic *and* tactical priority of every organization. Those who do it best will win the war.

Read on to learn how to develop talent management as a top strategy. Read on to discover simple but powerful ideas to improve your leadership recruitment process and new approaches in making your organization the best that it can be.

Acknowledgments

MY THANKS AND appreciation go to so many people it will not be possible to list them all. I have been so blessed to have worked in such fine organizations and so fortunate to have served such outstanding clients. Through the years I have worked with several individuals who clearly knew that finding and keeping strong leaders was the key to organizational success. These leaders showed me many of the valuable tips included in this book. I also appreciate all the fine examples that so many individuals who have joined me over the past twenty years in my various workshops and seminars have shared with me. Truly I often learn more about leadership excellence from them than they realize.

I would like to offer special thanks to Kam Sigafoos, Bill Sanger, Dr. Greg Taylor, Mike Covert, Gene Miyamoto, Steve Mickus, Susan Hunsaker, Dr. Ed Pike, Mike Gilligan, Mark Hannahan, Mark Elliott, and Randy Schimmoeller.

As with my prior books, I am very appreciative of the staff at Health Administration Press for their service to our healthcare industry. Audrey Kaufman was especially supportive. I must also make note of the contributions of my editor, Nancy Haiman, who was quite expert in her counsel and suggestions, and a joy to work with.

I have been closely connected with this great American health-care industry in some way since 1973—and I continue to find highly dedicated servant leaders, those who give so much to their organizations and community. I must recognize them and the service they provide. It was from many of them that I have learned so much. While I never felt I would finish one book, much less three, I simply must say that I live in the workshop and I am very observant. I hope these lessons will help other leaders excel.

I save my most important acknowledgment for last. My family continues to be my total purpose and strength in my life. My four daughters, Carly, Emily, Liesl, and Blakely, always allow me "time to write." My wife, Joaquina, my soulmate and best friend, also keeps me humble and strong. Liesl was also helpful in developing many of the illustrations and graphs in the book. I continue to be very blessed to have these five women uphold me and love me.

Introduction

"We are competing with every other organization out there for talent. It is scarce, it is expensive, and finding those people has never been more challenging."

—*Gary A. Mecklenburg, President and CEO*
Northwestern Memorial Hospital (Jaklevic 2000)

"There probably is a narrower list of candidates [for CEO] than you would have had a few years ago. It's not a situation where you can sit back in an easy chair and consider a long list."

—*Beth Ela Wilkens, Chair, Via Health (Jaklevic 2000)*

OVER THE PAST two to three years, an awareness of a shortage of leadership talent has begun to surface in most industries. In a recent article in the *Harvard Business Review,* Peter Cappelli, professor at the Wharton School, depicts the difficult nature of recruitment and retention in today's world. He describes the "intensity of the talent war" and indicates that because of the shortages, many companies today are hiring talent even when there are no vacancies, in effect stockpiling the talent. Cappelli (2000) states, "The signs of an explosion in outside hiring are everywhere. The open competition for other companies' people, once a rarity in business, is now an accepted fact." Other industries have been addressing the leadership shortage for several years.

In healthcare, however, the issue is just coming into focus. Although there is a keen awareness in healthcare of shortages of nurses, other professionals, and entry-level workers, the shortage

1

of leadership talent has not been quite as visible. Why? One reason is that the effect of the nursing and other staff shortages in hospitals is felt immediately. If a nursing unit does not have enough staff, it must turn to a temporary agency to fill the void. If this option is not able to meet the staffing need, a unit may have to be closed, which immediately affects services. In contrast, if a vice president–level position is open for weeks or months, other managers or executives generally can cover the bases that have the greatest effect on service delivery. New strategic directions may not be pursued during the interim, but basic services are not interrupted.

Another less obvious reason involves demographics. Healthcare leaders tend to be part of the baby-boom generation while healthcare workers tend to be part of the baby-bust generation. In the past, the supply of healthcare leaders has been sufficient to meet leadership needs. As the baby-boomers reach retirement age, this will no longer be the case. During the past decades, the number of leadership jobs in healthcare has increased dramatically. Executive positions, such as vice president of marketing, vice president of managed care, or vice president of legal services, were rare in healthcare organizations during the 1970s. As the industry grew, so did the need for new leadership positions.

Visibility of the healthcare leadership shortage is increasing significantly, as witnessed by the October 2, 2000 cover story in widely read *Modern Healthcare*. Titled "Wanted: A Few Good Leaders," the article stated, "At a time when they arguably need qualified executives the most, the nation's integrated delivery systems are encountering a shortage of skilled leaders" (Jaklevic 2000). The Healthcare Research and Development Institute, a think-tank organization that includes a number of top health system CEOs, reported that the pool of candidates with the appropriate skills and training for top leadership positions is now small (Jaklevic 2000).

Healthcare search consultants also describe the increased difficulty in finding candidates and the longer times required to complete search assignments. Mike Corey (2001), from search firm Witt Kieffer Ford Hadelman & Lloyd, stated, "Ten years ago, we were able to bring forward eight to nine strong candidates in a typical healthcare executive search; today, we do well to present five strong candidates."

Graduate health administration programs are also concerned about lower enrollments and declining leadership talent entering the field (AUPHA 2000). During the February 2001 National Summit on Education and Performance in Health Services Management and Policy, sponsored by the Association of University Programs in Health Administration and convened in Orlando, chairs of most of the graduate programs in health administration, almost 100 CEOs of healthcare organizations, and a number of search consultants voiced and discussed this concern.

Healthcare administration just does not seem to be as attractive as it once was. Perhaps fewer senior leaders spend time mentoring and encouraging young future leaders. Perhaps part-time MBA programs are attracting more future leaders than full-time health administration programs.

Many in healthcare are asking, "Where have all the leaders gone?" or, "Where are they all going?"

ABOUT THIS BOOK

This book addresses the challenge of ensuring the continued availability of talented, high-quality, high-performing healthcare leaders. At the leadership level, this poses an even greater challenge to the future of healthcare than staff shortages at other levels or perhaps any other issue. This book is about "talent management."

What is talent management? *Talent management* is a formal process for identifying, attracting, evaluating, recruiting, developing, and retaining leadership talent—the business of finding and recruiting managers and executives and moving them into organizations in a way that enables them to maximize their value to the organization. As one, if not *the* most important aspect of managing the organization, talent management involves the appropriate use of leaders within an organization.

Talent management reflects the ability of an organization to attract superior leaders. It also reflects the willingness and ability of the organization to turn superior leaders loose in an environment where they can reach peak performance in terms of patient or quality outcomes, physician and employee satisfaction, and financial return. Simply stated, talent management involves tapping the power and creativity of expert leaders. It is a movement away from mediocrity and toward excellence. If performed well, talent management will truly set great organizations apart from all others. See Figure I-1 for a graphic representation of the talent management model.

In its landmark study, "The War For Talent," McKinsey & Company (1998) captured the essence of this issue in contemporary U.S. business. The company's research indicated not only a shortage of highly effective leadership talent across many industries, but also that the top performing companies list talent management as one of their highest strategic priorities. "What emerged (from the study) is a wake-up call to corporate America," stated the report.

WHY THIS BOOK?

This book is designed to achieve two goals. The first is to serve as a "call to arms" for the leaders of American healthcare organizations to acknowledge the need for leadership talent and to focus more aggressively on its development and retention. It is directed to board members, chief executive officers, chief operating officers, chief human resources officers, and all senior executives who are involved with the recruitment and development of leadership talent. The book is designed to assist in defining and focusing on the issue of managing leadership talent and asks those involved to focus on recruiting and developing talent in such positions as chief

Figure I-1 Talent Management Model

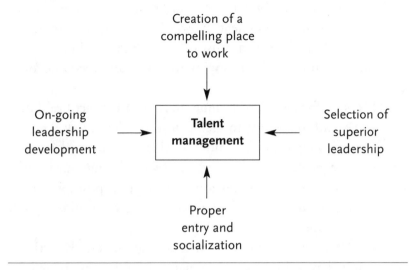

executive officer, chief operating officer, chief financial officer, vice president of medical administration, and all other senior leadership positions in hospitals and health systems. Secondly, the book presents specific strategies that organizations can use to identify, attract, recruit, retain, develop, and maximize superior management and executive talent.

Leaders of American hospitals, health systems, and other healthcare organizations can no longer afford to ignore the issue of talent management, the impending shortages of executive and management talent, and the need to place priority on leadership recruitment and development. These issues cannot be relegated to the human resources department as an annual project, nor can the initiatives simply be handed to search firms or management development consultants. Talent management must become the main concern of every healthcare organization, large and small, and must become part of the fabric or culture and a passion in every organization. Managing talent must become the job of every healthcare leader.

For years, leadership development in healthcare has focused on improving leaders' skills, competencies, and behaviors. The emphasis has been on building better organizations through leadership and management development. Now, with the critical shortage of leaders, the healthcare field must do much more to improve the environment in which leaders work to attract and retain talented executives.

This book focuses on techniques to find and attract healthcare executives and managers, to create cultures that allow them to excel, and to provide opportunities for them to grow and advance in their careers. Talent, of course, is needed throughout healthcare organizations in all professional and support positions; however, management of such talent across the organization is beyond this book's scope.

Jack Welch, recently retired president of General Electric, is often quoted as saying that his primary role in the company is to serve as the "people leader." He talks of constantly recruiting for leadership talent and the critical need for companies to focus on the development of managers (Slater 2000). "GE's success model is based in great part on its ability to hire great people and create a performance culture," noted Joe Hogan (2001), president of GE Medical Systems.

PREMISES

A number of premises form the basis for this book. A brief description of each follows.

- Demographic facts and day-to-day experience point to the shortage of leadership talent in many U.S. industries.
- The healthcare industry has been relatively isolated from leadership shortages until recently, but such shortages are now becoming evident.

- This leadership talent shortage will not disappear quickly, and in fact it is likely to become worse over the next decade. Demographics support this thesis. According to the Bureau of Labor Statistics (U.S. Department of Labor 2001), the group most likely to fill future leadership jobs—individuals age 25 to 44—is projected to decline to 44 percent of the labor force by 2008, from 51 percent in 1998. According to the U.S. Census Bureau (*Chief Executive* 2001), the most critical portion of this group—those age 35 to 44—is expected to decline 15 percent by 2015. Given the decline in these age groups, the demand for healthcare leaders will increase even more rapidly.

- Making a decision about the right leader is becoming tougher. Because individuals are more prepared for interviews and present themselves much more effectively than in the past, it has become more difficult to screen, evaluate, and discern among candidates. Outplacement firms that provide interview training have proliferated during the past 20 years. Networking is now used extensively by most candidates, providing candidates with multiple opportunities to practice marketing and selling themselves. Organizations such as the American College of Healthcare Executives offer many programs to help individuals prepare for their next job. The focus on presenting and selling yourself and preparing for the interview is now intense.

- The consequences of poor hiring decisions at the leadership level are much greater than they were in the past. Current profit margins are thinner. The industry is much more complex than it was and the pace of change and decision making has increased significantly. At the leadership level, it often takes longer to identify problems and concerns because they may be less tangible and visible. Moreover, the issues often involve interpersonal flaws that may not surface frequently or appear only when the leader is under pressure. Because of increased prevalence of employment contracts, severance payments, and litigation costs, the financial penalty of correcting hiring mistakes is more expensive than in the past. Whereas only 43 percent of hospitals offered CEOs an employment contract in 1989, this percentage had increased to nearly 60 percent by 1997 (ACHE 2000).

- Admitting you've made a hiring mistake is awkward and often very difficult. When hiring a leader, executives or managers "buy into" or endorse the new hire, creating a resistance to recognize a problem with the individual when it occurs. When those making the hiring decisions feel "ownership" of the decision, they may be slow to correct the mistake.

- New executives and managers do not have to "prove themselves" early in their tenure with the organization. Because leadership positions have longer orientation periods, errors in judgment take longer to surface. The decisions leaders make have more long-reaching consequences and take longer to assess. For example, if a leader makes poor decisions in selecting strategic directions, years may pass before those evaluating the leader can gauge the affect of those decisions. On the other hand, mistakes made by workers in entry level jobs usually can be spotted within the first few days or weeks.

- Because of the downsizing of some leadership teams, those remaining on the team may be stretched to their limits and experience significant stress. Some either leave the field or look for opportunities elsewhere, thereby increasing shortages of high-quality talent.

- Current healthcare leaders are aging along with the rest of the population. Many leaders report that in the next five years, more CEOs of acute care organizations will reach retirement age than in the previous 15 years. As the babyboom generation approaches retirement age, this trend is likely to become even more pronounced. Such significant senior-level turnover will, in domino fashion, create even further change and stress in the leadership ranks of American healthcare. The talent shortage is likely to be exacerbated by early retirement of current senior executives who have healthy retirement portfolios and supplemental retirement benefits.

OVERVIEW OF CONTENTS

Chapter 1, *The Leadership Challenge: Creating a Compelling Place for Leaders to Work,* opens with a call for making the talent management process a key strategic initiative at the board and senior management level and suggests general guidelines for beginning to address talent management. The chapter proposes that one of the best ways to win the war for talent is to create a compelling place for leaders to work. This is the book's cornerstone thesis. Developing the organizational elements that attract and retain highly successful leaders may be the most important step that an organization can take. Strategies for this development include allowing leaders to make a difference; pushing the organization to be dynamic and ever-changing; providing an ethical environment; creating teams of individuals with similar vision, commitment, and values; and emphasizing measurement and a goal orientation.

The next four chapters examine the process involved with selecting leadership talent. Chapter 2, *The Preparation Stage,* describes the steps completed well before any ad is placed or interview conducted. These steps include evaluating the need for the position, determining a search strategy, approaching the hiring process in a systematic manner, ensuring search process ownership and management, defining the job functions and qualifications, describing required and preferred attributes and competencies, and following the timetable for the selection process.

Chapter 3, *Sourcing to Find Superior Talent,* suggests ways to locate management and executive candidates. It describes finding talent (knowing how and where to reach candidates), attracting talent (knowing how to sell to those candidates), and screening talent (knowing which candidates merit additional discussion and review).

Chapter 4, *Interviewing and Evaluation,* suggests ways to improve the interview and evaluation process. These strategies include, among others, defining the interview's purpose, determining in advance who will interview and what their role will be, ensuring trained interviewers, allotting proper time for interviews, asking the tough questions, developing and using a written evaluation tool, creating rules to minimize bias during the interview process, and taking care of the candidate.

Chapter 5, *Making the Hiring Decision,* outlines key factors in an enhanced decision-making process. These factors include identifying critical elements of the selection decision, asking candidates for additional information, objectively evaluating prior work experience, conducting reference checks, obtaining and managing interview team input, evaluating candidates using decision criteria, making a selection decision, and extending an offer.

The next two chapters address how leadership talent can be maximized after an executive or manager is hired. Chapter 6, *Learning the Ropes,* describes the critical importance of how new leaders enter the organization, acclimate to it, and develop and pursue their leadership mandate. It outlines how to improve the entry and socialization process, from understanding the problems leaders face to being attentive to the new leader's social, community, and family needs.

Chapter 7, *Leadership Development,* provides practical guidance on how to improve leadership development. Strategies include developing a process for identifying future leaders, implementing a leadership development program, addressing higher level needs, involving senior leaders in the program's development, looking to other industries for development strategies, identifying leadership measures, creating opportunities for managers to expand the scope of their responsibility, providing the resources, and other developmental strategies.

The next three chapters describe different approaches to or structures for identifying and attracting leadership talent. Chapter 8, *Search Committees,* addresses the healthcare industry's unique use of organizational search committees and suggests ways to improve this approach. Suggestions include determining why a search committee is being used; appointing a process manager, the right chairperson, and committee members; developing a clear process and timetable; and defining roles and ground rules. It also describes use of search committees for physician executive positions, clinical and nursing executive positions, and medical department chairs or section chiefs.

Chapter 9, *Executive Search Firms,* examines the use of executive search firms and suggests ways to improve their use. It describes types of search firms, such as contingency firms and retained firms, reasons to use and not to use search firms, and outlines the employer's responsibility during the search process.

Chapter 10, *Assessments and Assessment Psychologists,* written by contributor Jared D. Lock, Ph.D., addresses the use of assessment tools and executive assessment psychologists in selecting leaders. It describes what assessments are and what should be measured when assessing executives. It outlines types of assessments and how to select high-quality psychologists and assessment tools.

Finally, the Epilogue, *Critical Lessons in Talent Management,* summarizes the goals critical to obtaining and keeping the very best leadership talent in healthcare.

"Evaluate Your Organization" sections appear at the end of each chapter. These summarize the key points and enable readers to evaluate their own organizations according to the parameters discussed in the chapters. Readers who work through these in depth will find the exercise valuable.

MAKING A DIFFERENCE

I have always suggested to those with whom I have worked and those who have spent time with me in the seminar room or the graduate classroom that healthcare is a very special industry. It is populated by many who chose their careers to serve others, to care for those less fortunate, and to make a difference in the organizations and communities in which they work and live. This is not just a grand statement of ideals; instead, it is lived out every day by leaders in small rural hospitals, in inner-city hospitals, and in hospitals and health systems of all sizes and types. Through my executive search work, I have had the chance to work with, teach, or recruit many of these people. This book is for and about them— those who place service at the forefront and those who minister through their leadership. For individuals entering this field seeking leadership positions, keep these ideals in mind and practice. For those who continue to serve during times of stress and great challenge, keep the faith. For those who are about to retire and begin other endeavors, we thank you for walking the path before us.

"Everything rises and falls on leadership. Whenever I make that statement the listeners are tempted to change it to, '*Almost* everything rise and falls on leadership.' Most people have a desire to look for the exception instead of the desire to become exceptional."

John C. Maxwell, Founder
The INJOY Group (1993)

REFERENCES

American College of Healthcare Executives. 2002. *Contracts for Healthcare Executives,* 4th ed. Chicago: ACHE.

Association of University Programs in Health Administration. 2000. Report of the AUPHA Task Force on Evidence-Based Management Education. January. Washington, DC: AUPHA.

Cappelli, P. 2000. "A Market-Driven Approach to Retaining Talent." *Harvard Business Review* January/February: 103–113.

Chief Executive. 2002. "CE Roundtable: The War for Talent." [Online article; retrieved 1/4/02]. http://www.chiefexecutive.net/round/rtwar.htm.

Corey, M. 2001. Witt Kieffer Ford Hadelman & Lloyd. Personal conversation, April.

Hogan, J. 2001. "Leadership at GE." Presented at the National Summit on Education and Performance in Health Services Management and Policy, Orlando, FL, February 8–10.

Jaklevic, M.C. 2000. "Wanted: A Few Good Leaders." *Modern Healthcare* 30(41): 38–40.

Maxwell, J.C. 1993. *Developing the Leader Within You*. Nashville, TN: Thomas Nelson Publishers, ii.

McKinsey & Company. 1998. "The War for Talent." *The McKinsey Quarterly* 3 (December): 44–57.

Slater, R. 2000. *The GE Way Fieldbook*. New York: McGraw-Hill, 33–38.

U.S. Department of Labor. 2000–2001. *Occupational Outlook Handbook*. Washington, DC: Bureau of Labor Statistics. http://stats.bls.gov/oco/oco2003.htm.

CHAPTER 1

The Leadership Challenge: Creating a Compelling Place for Leaders to Work

"Many American companies are already suffering a shortage of executive talent. Three-quarters of corporate officers surveyed said their companies had 'insufficient talent sometimes" or were "chronically talent-short across the board'."

—*McKinsey & Company, 1998*

IN THE *MCKINSEY QUARTERLY* article quoted above, the authors indicate that, "Companies are about to be engaged in a war for senior executive talent that will remain a defining characteristic of their competitive landscape for decades to come. Yet most are ill prepared, and even the best are vulnerable" (McKinsey & Company 1998). As stated in the Introduction, healthcare executive recruiters describe shortages of leadership talent at both the executive and middle-management level. Assuming that finding and retaining talent are such significant challenges, what steps will the more successful organizations take to address it? How will they prepare for it?

Commitment to talent management begins at the most senior level of the organization. This includes both the board and the CEO. A description of the key commitments the board, CEO, and other senior leaders should make follows.

ADOPT TALENT MANAGEMENT AS A
KEY STRATEGIC INITIATIVE

Talent management must become a passion for all senior leaders, beginning with the board and CEO—it is *not* simply a job for the human resources department. Healthcare CEO Michael Covert (2001) commented, "The recruitment of accomplished leaders is one of the most important things that can be done to improve an organization." Dick Vague (2001), CEO of First USA, stated, "I have been personally involved in hiring everyone in the top management group, and many three or four levels below that. If it's the most important thing, your calendar reflects it." Norm Nicholson (2001), a board chair of a successful Midwestern health system, stated, "We must find the best leadership talent to ensure our long-range successes."

Recruiting and retaining the best leadership talent is accomplished by making talent management one of the key initiatives on the corporate agenda. The board of trustees must understand and support an emphasis on talent management from a governance standpoint. It must make winning the war for talent a top priority and support aggressive and creative ways to develop leaders, compensation strategies, and other activities. Along with financial and quality indicators, boards should review leadership indicators of performance, such as measures of leadership retention and development. Talent management must be an item that merits frequent discussion and action plans at the senior management table. The discussions and plans must include all aspects of working with talent, from recruitment and selection to development and support for growth. As described later in this book, talent management involves developing a specific measure of success and holding leaders accountable for both their own and others' performance. The board and CEO must fully embrace performance measurement.

Finally, senior leaders must buy into and create what McKinsey & Company calls an "employee value proposition." These propositions

—such as the vision and values shared by an organization's senior leadership team—are the compelling reasons why leadership talent is attracted to an organization and stays employed by the organization.

STUDY AND UNDERSTAND TALENT MANAGEMENT AS A *PROCESS*

Senior leadership teams of the most successful organizations realize that talent management is a process. They have given significant thought to what talent management is and how they will manage it. These leaders include it as a responsibility of *all* management, from the CEO to middle managers. A description of the leadership role in the chief components of the talent management process follows.

Commit to the concept of creating a compelling place for leaders to work

Perhaps more than any other process element, this activity, when ongoing, makes the organization truly effective. Organizations that do this well often realize an additional benefit—they become well known in the industry and therefore do not have to exert as much recruiting effort when seeking outside talent. Much of this chapter is devoted to this critical topic of commitment.

Design and implement a more effective leadership hiring methodology

Leaders in organizations that are most successful at talent management approach the hiring process with a passion. They know room always exists to improve their process for interviewing, selecting, and orienting managers and executives. These leaders develop, implement, and fine tune a formal approach to management and executive recruiting. Accountability and time frames are established and monitored for each step.

Make the hiring process more selective

The senior leadership team in highly successful organizations is very particular about who it hires. The team spends a great deal of effort interviewing, evaluating, and assessing candidates. The team sets very aggressive standards regarding who fits and who does not and expends great effort to assess this. According to Edward L. Gubman (1998), Global Practice Leader for Hewitt Associates, "Selective hiring means a long-term employment relationship for people who fit."

Making the hiring process more selective also tends to create a higher satisfaction level for managers and executives. Several hospitals and companies have also shown the high correlation between management, staff, and patient satisfaction levels. An excellent example from retail comes from Sears. Rucci, Kim, and Quinn (1998) describe how Sears made significant changes in its culture and was able to "track success from management behavior through employee attitudes to customer satisfaction and financial performance."

Improve the manner in which new leaders are assimilated, oriented, and socialized

Senior leaders in effective organizations place a high value on helping new managers and executives enter and integrate into the organization. They understand the stress involved with taking a new leadership position and moving to a new community.

*Create and manage leadership expectations and move
nonperformers and marginal performers out of the organization*

Recent work by McKinsey & Company (2001) indicates that moving marginally performing leaders out of the organization is one
of the most important factors in retaining high performing leaders. The talent management process includes a strong commitment to *measuring* progress and taking appropriate action if goals
are not achieved. Senior leaders in the most effective organizations
are quantitative and pursue measurement vigorously.

Support developmental opportunities for managers and executives

Leadership development must be a priority. The most successful
organizations are those that offer regular educational opportunities for growth and development. This means much more than
simply classes. It involves developing an environment that offers
mentoring, random educational "learning moments," and chances
to work on projects that fall outside of traditional functional
boundaries. These opportunities include providing financial support for travel to educational conferences so that leaders may network and study best practices.

Develop a succession planning program

Succession planning is the formal process an organization uses
to catalog, inventory and manage the replacement of its top leaders through development, education, coaching, and experiential
programs. It involves studying each leadership position in the
organization, determining the potential of the incumbent to
leave or move up within the organization, and identifying developmental and educational needs for various individuals across

the organization. In addition to targeted retention strategies, this process may involve coaching, rotation to different jobs, and providing new and varied experiences.

In the past, healthcare organizations have not done succession planning well. To gain greater responsibilities, healthcare leaders usually have to move to other organizations because internal promotional opportunities are scarce. Healthcare organizations are often too small to offer the traditional "management training" positions available in other industries where up-and-coming leaders are rotated through multiple areas of the company, such as finance, human resources, and marketing, receiving along the way a broad exposure to the company's operations. Healthcare should not be discouraged by the difficulty of providing broader exposure to its leaders. Strategies for doing so are covered fully in chapter 7.

UNDERSTAND THAT TALENT MANAGEMENT IS ABOUT MUCH MORE THAN JUST COMPENSATION

Many senior leaders believe that money is the most important issue in attracting and retaining top-notch executive talent. They believe that they have the talent management issue "handled" because the organization's management and executive salaries are in the 75th percentile and because they link pay to performance through both incentive compensation programs and merit-based pay increases. Taking comfort in this approach has two primary weaknesses.

First, research conducted by Peter Capelli at the Wharton School indicates that there is always another company in the market that will poach or lure away the very best talent with a higher price. According to Capelli (2001), there is no way to completely isolate talent from a higher offer in the market: "You have to accept the new reality: The market, not your company, will ultimately determine the movement of your employees. You can't shield your people from attractive opportunities and aggressive recruiters."

Edward L. Gubman (1998), a widely-recognized compensation consultant cited earlier, states, "Yet competing for employees primarily through higher compensation never has been enough to attract and retain the best talent." Gubman proposes that the individuals organizations really want to employ in leadership positions look for more from their work than just pay. This touches on the second problem—a focus on money ignores reams of academic and practical research that shows that many other factors relate to a leader's desire to come to and remain with an organization. Among these are a drive for achievement, the desire to serve, and the satisfaction of working with a leadership team with similar values and vision.

According also to Gubman (1998), "Companies with strong cultures pick people who fit their cultures. They recognize that technical, interpersonal, and problem-solving skills are not enough for a successful hire. People have to fit the values. People who don't fit need to find employment elsewhere."

CREATE A COMPELLING PLACE FOR LEADERS TO WORK

An obvious solution to the talent shortage at leadership levels is to develop an organization to which the very best and brightest leaders will want to come and stay. Under a well-known national program sponsored by the American Nurses Association, some hospitals have chosen to develop themselves into "magnet hospitals." The magnet hospital program identifies the key elements that attract and retain professional nurses, the factors that make an environment a positive one in which to work (see www.nursingworld.org/ancc/magnet.htm). Creating in a similar fashion a compelling place for healthcare leaders to work may be the best way to find and retain executive and management talent.

Interestingly, the management literature is full of books and articles telling *what* leadership is, describing *how* to do it better, or espousing the latest leadership trends. Stephen Covey's popular book, *The 7 Habits of Highly Effective People* (1989), captivated Americans as they tried to apply his principles to their lives. Peter Scholtes' book, *The Leader's Handbook: Making Things Happen, Getting Things Done* (1998), described many day-to-day practical tips for improving leadership. My recent book, *Leadership in Healthcare: Values At The Top* (2000) provided a wide-ranging discussion of leadership issues. Yet very few books seem to indicate exactly what it is that highly effective leaders want in an organization.

Two books have addressed this issue from the perspective of the rank-and-file employee. They are *The 100 Best Companies to Work for in America* by Robert Levering, Milton Moskowitz, and Michael Katz (1994) and *A Great Place to Work: What Makes Some Employers So Good—And Most So Bad* by Robert Levering (1988). Levering (1988) concludes, "From an employee viewpoint, a great workplace is one in which you trust the people you work for, have pride in what you do, and enjoy the people you are working with."

Developing a "leadership-friendly" environment sounds easy enough. Simply determine what highly effective leaders want from an organization, develop those attributes organizationwide, and then the recruitment and retention of highly effective leaders becomes effortless. By studying the characteristics of organizations that seem to attract highly effective leaders, one should be able simply to inculcate these attributes into an organization's culture.

It is not so simple. Defining what leaders want from an organization requires further research. To address this information gap, I interviewed several individuals known for their leadership effectiveness in healthcare to learn what they seek in organizations. I asked the following questions:

- What are the characteristics a great organization needs to attract and retain highly effective leaders?
- What do strong leaders look for in a work setting?

- What type of environment provides the best climate or culture for successful executives and managers?

Several key themes emerged. To summarize, organizations that are successful in attracting and retaining superior talent

- have a clear mission and vision;
- are dynamic and exciting;
- provide the opportunity for leaders to make a difference in the work they do;
- provide an ethical environment, both in purpose and practice;
- allow leaders to grow intellectually as well as in responsibility level;
- give leaders the chance to work with others who have a shared vision, commitment, and values;
- strive to create an effective and disciplined environment; and
- emphasize goals and measurement of goal attainment.

A well-known book, *Built To Last: Successful Habits of Visionary Companies* by James Collins and Jerry Porras (1994), also provides insight into the attributes that high-quality leaders wish to find in organizations. According to the authors, strong companies:

- practice clock building, not time-telling;
- are interested in more than profits;
- preserve the core while stimulating progress;
- pursue big, hairy, audacious goals (BHAGs);
- have cult-like cultures;
- try a lot of stuff and keep what works;
- practice home-grown management;
- believe that good enough never is;
- ensure alignment, meaning that all of the component parts of the company work together to move toward the company's vision; and
- build the vision.

Although their studies did not include healthcare organizations, the lessons learned are applicable.

Based on the information outlined above, the following goals should be pursued to create a healthcare organization that attracts and retains highly successful leaders.

Create a clear vision and mission

Strong leaders are naturally attracted to organizations whose vision and mission are unequivocal and unambiguous. Individuals working in these organizations know why the organizations exist. They develop a clarity about what they are doing. A consistent excitement of purpose is alive and well throughout the organization. Much more than a written mission statement on the walls of the organization, highly successful healthcare organizations are marked by a passion for what they do. There is no confusion about what needs to be done and little conflict about how to get there. The directions, goals, and objectives required to meet the mission and vision seem so obvious.

Often, it is helpful to look outside the hospital/health system world to see excellence of vision and mission in practice. A closely-related company, pharmaceutical giant Merck & Company, states its mission as "We are in the business of preserving and improving human life. All of our actions must be measured by our success in this goal." Johnson & Johnson, well known for its positive leadership during the 1982 Tylenol crisis, has a well-developed and explicit mission statement. See Figure 1.1 for Johnson & Johnson's credo. Healthcare leaders may wish to compare their statements to this one to determine if the statements are specific enough and understandable. They also may want to determine the real value and merit of their mission statements. To be valuable, the statements must permeate organizationwide decision making.

Figure 1.1 Johnson & Johnson's Credo

We believe our first responsibility is to the doctors, nurses and patients,
to mothers and fathers and all others who use our products and services.
In meeting their needs everything we do must be of high quality.
We must constantly strive to reduce our costs
in order to maintain reasonable prices.
Customers' orders must be serviced promptly and accurately.
Our suppliers and distributors must have an opportunity
to make a fair profit.

We are responsible to our employees,
the men and women who work with us throughout the world.
Everyone must be considered as an individual.
We must respect their dignity and recognize their merit.
They must have a sense of security in their jobs.
Compensation must be fair and adequate,
and working conditions clean, orderly and safe.
We must be mindful of ways to help our employees fulfill
their family responsibilities.
Employees must feel free to make suggestions and complaints.
There must be equal opportunity for employment, development
and advancement for those qualified.
We must provide competent management,
and their actions must be just and ethical.

We are responsible to the communities in which we live and work
and to the world community as well.
We must be good citizens—support good works and charities
and bear our fair share of taxes.
We must encourage civic improvements and better health and education.
We must maintain in good order
the property we are privileged to use,
protecting the environment and natural resources.

Our final responsibility is to our stockholders.
Business must make a sound profit.

(continued)

Figure 1.1 *(continued)*

We must experiment with new ideas.
Research must be carried on, innovative programs developed
and mistakes paid for.
New equipment must be purchased, new facilities provided
and new products launched.
Reserves must be created to provide for adverse times.
When we operate according to these principles,
the stockholders should realize a fair return.

Source: Johnson & Johnson. 2001. Corporate communication.

Allow leaders to make a difference

Highly successful leaders are interested not only in change, but in making a difference. They pursue change to make a positive contribution rather than for change's sake. Highly effective leaders constantly seek out flaws and implement positive change to improve their organization in part, and society as a whole (Dye 2000). One of the distinguishing characteristics of the finest healthcare leaders is the fact that they chose the healthcare field because of its remarkable contribution to society. Because a large proportion of healthcare organizations have a not-for-profit status, their leaders often are committed to "giving back to the community." For example, a number of inner-city healthcare organizations, surrounded by poor neighborhoods, work with their local banks to encourage the banks to provide low-interest loans to healthcare employees. Such loans enable employees to live close to their jobs and to fix up houses in the organization's immediate vicinity, thereby improving the quality of the neighborhood. This differs significantly from the opposite strategy, which is to put up walls, gates, and fences to "keep out the bad people."

Push the organization to be dynamic and ever-changing

Effective organizations address change positively as a day-to-day certainty. Excitement always exists about the next project or venture. Change management programs are embraced as a way of life and bureaucracy is nonexistent. Historically, many hospitals developed pervasive and bureaucratic policies, rules, and standards in an effort to create a "no mistakes, no errors" culture, which often stifled creativity and innovation. Bureaucracy is not just a characteristic of large organizations; it is found in all sizes and types of organizations. General Electric, one of the largest corporations in the world, and one that many would expect to have a huge bureaucracy, is instead known for eliminating internal bureaucratic rules and regulations. Former CEO Jack Welch said, "We have to weed out bureaucracies before they become jungles. Bureaucracies will eat you alive. Let's keep our organizational structure simple and let people take their own initiative. We want autonomy and entrepreneurship. We also want to be better than the best" (Vance and Deacon 1995).

An important point associated with this is the need to allow and encourage the practice of flexible leadership. In a dynamic environment, the most effective leaders employ a variety of leadership styles and approaches. In his article, "Leadership That Gets Results," Daniel Goleman (2000) identifies six distinct leadership styles: coercive, authoritative, affiliative, democratic, pacesetting, and coaching. "The research indicates that leaders with the best results do not rely on only one leadership style. They use most of them in a given week—seamlessly and in different measure—dependent on the business situation," writes Goleman. A number of healthcare executives practice varied styles of leadership. One southern CEO was known for her ability to move seamlessly from a coaching style to an affiliative style to an authoritative style. She frequently used the coaching style with junior executives and the affiliative style with medical staff members, and yet had the ability to be authoritative when the organization needed clear and decisive leadership.

Provide an ethical environment

Highly effective leaders are attracted to organizations that are very ethical both in purpose and practice. The leaders' values *require* that they work in a highly ethical environment. Ethical organizations have well-defined expectations for leaders in terms of vendor relationships, avoiding conflicts of interest, and expense reimbursement. When potential problems surface in these organizations, the issues are addressed promptly rather than swept under the rug. Corporate compliance programs exist in such organizations not because they are required, but because the programs are the right thing to have. A number of faith-based organizations do an excellent job of turning traditional corporate compliance programs into positive attributes of their organizational culture. They show why it is right to do the right things, and inculcate these principles throughout their educational, orientation, and performance assessment programs.

Allow leaders to grow intellectually and gain responsibly

Strong leaders are life-long learners. They are curious and interested in studying best practices and other approaches to issues and problems. Organizations that attract and retain strong leaders have a vigorous commitment to continuing education and make provisions for leaders to gain new skills and exposure. This commitment goes far beyond simply providing support for formal classes; these organizations also develop an environment that nourishes curiosity and feeds knowledge. Leadership teams spend time discussing trends and exploring new ideas and concepts.

Additionally, effective organizations provide leaders with an opportunity for additional responsibility. When vacancies occur, existing team members have the chance to assume additional roles with new departments or programs. Some organizations provide the opportunity for job rotation which involves different executives trading departmental accountabilities. Several large healthcare organizations move junior-level executives from one functional area to another, preparing them for future moves to higher-level positions.

Create teams of individuals with similar vision, commitment, and values

Highly effective organizations expend great effort creating senior leadership teams that include members with similar values, principles, and visions. The sharing of values and visions provides team members with camaraderie and a spirited environment in which to work. Unfortunately, many leadership teams in American healthcare organizations are comprised of individuals who value only their own efforts—team endeavors are discouraged. Highly effective leaders cannot tolerate this type of culture. Instead, they love to work in groups, sharing ideas, sparring over the best solutions to problems, and sharing the glory of accomplishments. "Those who believe in dignity, meaning, and community and who want to create the hundred and first best place to work must somehow, some way, involve everybody," wrote author Weisbord (1987) referring to *The 100 Best Companies to Work for in America.*

Procter & Gamble (P&G) is well known for teamwork and turning teams loose to pursue entrepreneurial endeavors. Collins and Porras (1994) stated that "P&G people feel proud to be part of an organization that describes itself as special, great, excellent, moral, self-disciplined, full of the best people, an institution, and unique among the world's business organizations." Working for organizations with national and international reputations, such as the Cleveland Clinic, Mayo Clinic, or Johns Hopkins, gives individuals a certain feeling of pride and helps cement teams together. Recognition in the various "top 100" hospital lists also provides an opportunity for organizations to build staff morale. Healthcare organizations that may not be as well known can also help their employees develop feelings of pride that strengthen leadership team bonds. Sharing the results of successful performance improvement initiatives, for example, can enhance leadership and staff morale.

Emphasize measurement and goal orientation

Successful managers and executives assess results against established objectives and targets and enjoy having their accomplishments measured. According to Gubman (1998), "Measurement changes everything. All elements of alignment and engagement become more urgent and useful when you start to measure their outcomes. If you aren't prepared to measure the results of these processes, they may not be worth doing. If you don't measure, you won't know or understand the results you are achieving." Objectives usually are tied directly to goals in the organization's strategic plan, enabling leaders to see where they have made a difference.

In essence, successful organizations are increasingly outcome-oriented. A number of well-known healthcare organizations have adopted the balanced scorecard and other approaches to performance improvement and management. Even during the recent difficult times of financial pressure due to the Balanced Budget Act, several hospitals and health systems were able to stay ahead of the challenge by setting specific targets and measuring progress toward these targets on an ongoing basis.

At the same time, successful leaders hold all other managers in the organization accountable to a defined set of objectives. One Midwestern health system CEO put it this way: "If we hold ourselves accountable for measurable objectives at the senior management level, it is only appropriate to expect the same at other levels in the organization." This means moving average-performing managers out of the organization. As mentioned earlier, one of the greatest sources of dissatisfaction for highly effective leaders is allowing average leaders to remain within the organization. The importance of removing average leaders cannot be over-emphasized. At GE, Jack Welch spoke of three kinds of managers (Slater 2000):

- Type As which should be kept, promoted, and rewarded;
- Type Bs which should be nurtured in the hope that they may become As; and
- Type Cs which should be dismissed as quickly as possible because trying to turn them into Bs or As isn't worth the time.

Welch's style of management gets to the very core of effectively running an enterprise. Keeping average or mediocre leaders is not fair to the organization and does not demonstrate effective leadership.

Concluding Comments

The best companies are those that concentrate on the key characteristics that keep highly effective leaders satisfied. A high satisfaction level is often contagious, moving downward to other staff within the organization and outward to the physicians and other stakeholders who work with the organization.

Figure 1.2 demonstrates the organizational elements that attract strong leaders. Note that the model is circular in nature—each element feeds the next. The organization that has a clear vision and mission allows leaders to believe they are making a difference. When this occurs, organizations are constantly changing. As they change, they need to function ethically and support their leaders in continuing to grow and work with others. In the end, measurement against established goals illustrates progress toward achieving the vision and mission.

Figure 1.2 Organizational Elements That Attract Strong Leaders

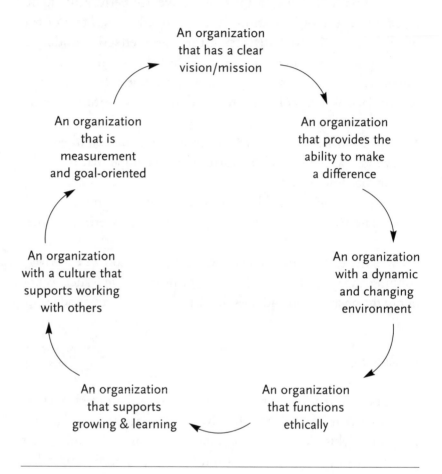

An organization
that has a clear
vision/mission

An organization
that is
measurement
and goal-oriented

An organization
that provides the
ability to make
a difference

An organization
with a culture that
supports working
with others

An organization
with a dynamic
and changing
environment

An organization
that supports
growing & learning

An organization
that functions
ethically

EVALUATE YOUR ORGANIZATION

1. Our board discusses the successes and failures of management and executive hiring.

Never   Infrequently   At Times   Frequently   On a Regular
Basis

2. Our senior leadership team has considered what makes the organization a compelling place for leaders to work.

Not at All	To a Small Extent	Somewhat	To a Great Extent	Totally and Completely

3. Our board has routine discussions about talent management issues.

Never	Infrequently	At Times	Frequently	On a Regular Basis

4. A formal and methodical process is in place to attract, hire, develop, and retain leadership talent.

Not at All	To a Small Extent	Somewhat	To a Great Extent	Totally and Completely

5. There are ample developmental opportunities for managers and executives.

Strongly Disagree	Disagree	Neither Disagree or Agree	Agree	Strongly Agree

6. Management and executive compensation receives the proper attention (not too much, not too little) within the organization.

Strongly Disagree	Disagree	Neither Disagree or Agree	Agree	Strongly Agree

7. Our senior leaders discuss what attracts strong leaders to our organization.

Not at All	To a Small Extent	Somewhat	To a Great Extent	Totally and Completely

8. Our board is committed to recruiting and retaining strong leaders.

Not at All	To a Small Extent	Somewhat	To a Great Extent	Totally and Completely

9. The organization's environment provides leaders with the following (rate each one):

- Clear vision and mission
- An opportunity to make a difference
- Support for change
- Support of the practice of flexible leadership styles
- Ethical environment
- Growth opportunities
- Team atmosphere
- Measurement and goal orientation

Not at All	To a Small Extent	Somewhat	To a Great Extent	Totally and Completely

REFERENCES

Cappelli, P. 2000. "A Market-Driven Approach to Retaining Talent." *Harvard Business Review* January/February: 103–113.

Covert, M. 2001. Personal communication. March.

Covey, S.R. 1989. *The 7 Habits of Highly Effective People.* New York: Simon and Schuster.

Dye, C.F. 2000. *Leadership in Healthcare: Values at the Top.* Chicago: Health Administration Press.

Goleman, D. 2000. "Leadership That Gets Results." *Harvard Business Review* March/April: 78–93.

Gubman, E.L. 1998. *The Talent Solution*. New York: McGraw-Hill, 63, 135, 292.

Johnson & Johnson. 2001. Corporate communication.

Levering, R. 1988. *A Great Place to Work: What Makes Some Employers So Good—And Most So Bad*. New York: Random House. Out of print.

Levering, R., Katz, M., and M. Moskowitz. 1994. *The 100 Best Companies to Work for in America*. New York: Plume.

McKinsey & Company. 1998. "The War for Talent." *The McKinsey Quarterly* 3 (December): 44–57.

———. 2001. "War for Talent." Presentation to the Healthcare Roundtable of Chief Executive Officers, February 15, Scottsdale, Arizona.

Nicholson, N. 2001. Personal communication, July.

Rucci, A.S., S.P. Kim, and R.T. Quinn. 1998. "The Employee-Customer-Profit Chain at Sears." *Harvard Business Review* January/February: 83.

Scholtes, P.R. 1998. *The Leader's Handbook: Making Things Happen, Getting Things Done*. New York: McGraw-Hill Professional Publishing.

Slater, R. 2000. *The GE Way Fieldbook*. New York: McGraw-Hill, 40.

Vague, D. 2001. Personal communication, March.

Vance, M., and D. Deacon. 1995. *Think Out of the Box*. Franklin Lakes, NJ: Career Press, 171.

Weisbord, M.R. 1987. *Productive Workplaces*. San Francisco: Jossey-Bass, 1.

SELECTING

LEADERSHIP

TALENT

CHAPTER 2

The Preparation Stage

"[According to Sorcher] one-third of those chosen for senior executive positions are subsequently seen as disappointments. Anecdotal information given to the Center for Creative Leadership suggest the number may be as high as 50 percent."

—*R. P. White and D. L. DeVries, 1990*

"You have a workforce strategy when you take a planned approach to acquiring, deploying, developing, and retaining talent."

—*E. L. Gubman, 1998*

MANY ORGANIZATIONS VENTURE into executive and management hiring in a haphazard manner, giving very little forethought to the process. Although the leaders' intentions are to focus intensively on beginning and successfully completing the search, the actual execution often is sloppy. Key problems include:

- Failure to prepare for the search by adequately defining needs, expectations, and qualifications;
- Failure to plan for and maintain steady progress; and
- Subjective decision making.

The speed of the search process often vacillates, starting quickly but losing momentum just as quickly. As other priorities surface, the recruitment process often is put on the back burner for a while. This results in lost candidates and disheartened internal candidates who feel that the organization does not value the job's importance. Such variability of momentum is usually a result of the lack of systematic and organized preparation or a lack of prioritization.

Hiring decisions often are made based on a "gut-feel." Whether called fit, chemistry, or jell, this gut feeling usually is not well defined. Many executive hiring processes are often little more than an endurance test focused almost exclusively on interpersonal style and fit. Candidates who make it through the first round of interviews without making significant interpersonal mistakes are often brought back for the second round.

Biases often exist in the interview process. Many psychologists suggest that what is observed in an interview is most often the personality or identity that a candidate wants and allows the interviewer to see. Greater preparation for the recruiting and interview process can minimize such bias. Selection psychologists Robert and Joyce Hogan (1992) described the interview challenge as follows:

> The word "personality" has two meanings. On the one hand, it refers to structures inside a person that are known primarily by that person and only inferred by others; this is personality from the perspective of the actor. On the other hand, personality refers to the distinctive impression that a person makes on others; this is personality from the perspective of the observer. Personality from the observer's perspective is essentially the same as a person's reputation. In order to measure personality, it is helpful to focus on those aspects that are observable—so that the measurement claims can be verified by others. The most observable part of personality is that which is known by others—a person's reputation.

Determining which candidate best fits a job or an organization is made more difficult by the nature of how people present themselves in interviews. Relying solely on personal interviews to select executives and managers without adequate and in-depth preparation on the front end will often lead to significant hiring mistakes.

IMPROVING THE PREPARATION STAGE

Healthcare organizations can pursue nine key strategies to improve the preparation stage. A description of each follows and a graphic representation of the process appears as Figure 2-1.

Evaluate the need for the position

First and foremost, determine whether the position is needed. Why was it created in the past? Although the need for many healthcare leadership positions, such as chief financial officer (CFO), inside legal counsel, CEO, and others may be very clear, the need for some positions may be less clear in terms of functions and roles.

For example, one organization may not need both a vice president of patient care services and a vice president of clinical services. A single individual might be able to fulfill all responsibilities. Or, one organization may not need an executive-level public relations position because a departmental director-level position may suffice. Some larger organizations have multiple vice presidents in the same functional areas, for example, a senior vice president of finance, a vice president of finance, a vice president of revenue cycle management, and so forth. This type of structure may not only be top heavy and redundant, but may also create organizational inequities. Matters described in these examples are best addressed immediately when a vacancy occurs rather than when the search to fill the vacancy has commenced.

Determine a search strategy

Given a need for the position, the next step is to decide if a search is necessary. Are there internal candidates who could immediately take over the jobs and tasks? Could the responsibilities be divided

Figure 2.1 Improving Selection Through Better Preparation

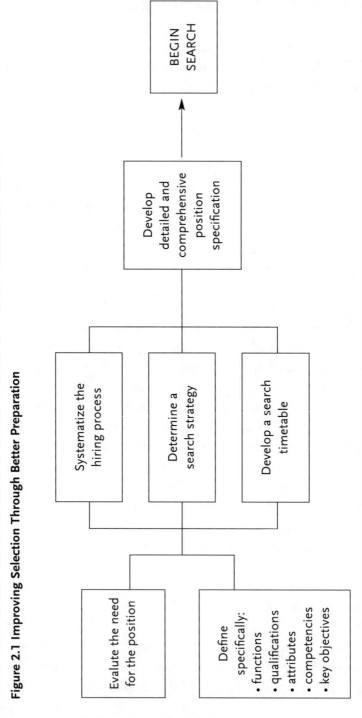

among other managers or executives? Could some or all of the job be outsourced? For example, if the executive responsible for billing services for housekeeping, dietary, maintenance, laundry, and other areas leaves the organization, it may be more appropriate to outsource those functions to a billing services firm with expertise in these areas. Some healthcare organizations also contract with external companies to provide leadership in various clinical areas such as physical therapy or pharmacy.

If an external search should be conducted, the organization's leaders must determine how quickly the position needs to be filled. They also must evaluate the prospect of interim leadership and determine who needs to be in the decision loop and who needs to merely provide input. For example, when a vice president of nursing vacancy occurs, input should be sought from key medical staff members even though the position reports directly to a chief operating officer. Input from key board members should almost always be sought with a CFO vacancy.

When discussing who should be in the decision loop and who should provide input, the senior leadership team must determine whether an individual will be given veto power over a candidate. Should any executive team member have the right to veto the selection of a candidate that he or she dislikes even if the position does not report directly to him or her? A leadership team may determine that the chief operating officer (COO), for example, should be given total veto authority over the human resources vice president candidates even though the position reports to the CEO.

Consider the potential problems and barriers that can block a successful search. For example, perhaps the CFO or another executive is not comfortable with the selection of a particular executive. The CFO may not be as cooperative with the incoming executive, thereby presenting a barrier or challenge to the individual's ability to perform his or her job. Or, salaries may provide a stumbling block. Discussions about and determination of a compensation package well in advance of beginning the search are critical to the search strategy. Many good candidates have been lost because the leadership team waits until the last minute to identify a salary level. When the preferred candidate indicates that he or she will not join the organization based on the given salary, the team then spends weeks trying to work out ways around the salary ceiling.

Approach the hiring process in a systematic manner

Have a method and a structure in place for the entire process. Critical steps and practices should be detailed and outlined. A framework for the entire process should be organized and logical. It should include decision points, timetables, and assignment of responsibilities. Figure 2.1 is a sample timetable for an organization conducting the search process on its own. Figure 2.2 is a timetable for an organization using a search firm. As a comparison of the two timetables illustrates, searches using a search firm often move more rapidly because an outside process manager focuses solely on completing the search.

Be certain that someone owns and manages the process

Whether the CEO, department head, the human resources vice president, or a search consultant, a single individual must captain the process of hiring an executive or a manager. For searches below the CEO level, the chief human resources officer typically manages the search process in healthcare organizations. If this person does not have the time or expertise, organizations typically turn to search firms. When the person being recruited is a CEO, a process manager is even more critical. It obviously would be inappropriate for a vice president–level executive to captain the CEO recruitment process. A board member may be appropriate, but often board members do not have the time or expertise to manage a recruitment process. In such cases, the board frequently turns

Figures 2.2 Timetable for a Successful Search (without the use of a search firm)

Month 1	Month 2	Month 3	Month 4	Month 5
Week 1 2 3 4	Week 1 2 3 4	Week 1 2 3 4	Week 1 2 3 4	Week 1 2 3 4

- Position need evaluated
- Function determined

- Search strategy determined
- Position specification written

- Ads, other sourcing
- Candidates identified and screened

- Candidates interviewed first round

- Candidates interviewed second round
- Finalists selected
- Final reference checks

- Evaluation
- Final discussion

- Preferred candidate selected
- Negotiations
- Executive hired

Reprinted, with permission, from Witt/Kieffer Ford Hadelman & Lloyd; published on their website, www.wittkieffer.com; and, reprinted, with permission, from Witt/Kieffer Ford Hadelman & Lloyd, marketing literature.

The Preparation Stage 45

Figure 2.3 Timetable for a Successful Search (with the use of a search firm)

	Month 1				Month 2				Month 3				Month 4			
	Week				Week				Week				Week			
	1	2	3	4	1	2	3	4	1	2	3	4	1	2	3	4

• Search firm selected

• Consultant evaluates organization
• Position criteria established

• Candidates identified and screened

• Consultant interviews candidates

• Consultant recommends candidates
• Client selects finalists for local interviews

• Client-candidate interviews

• Preferred candidate selected
• Negotiations
• Executive hired

Reprinted, with permission, from Witt/Kieffer Ford Hadelman & Lloyd; published on their website, www.wittkieffer.com; and, reprinted, with permission, from Witt/Kieffer Ford Hadelman & Lloyd. marketing literature.

to search consultants to manage the entire search process. Boards of smaller hospitals often try to manage the search process themselves because they do not want to pay search fees. In some cases, there may be a retired board member who can mange the process; in other cases, a savvy human resource executive on the board from another industry can manage the process. It is safe to estimate that 95 percent of the healthcare organizations with revenues of $100 million or more (constituting approximately 70 percent of all U.S. hospitals) use search firms for their CEO searches when an outside search is conducted.

Define the job functions in more detail

Job functions are the specific tasks and responsibilities that the person in the job must perform. Some are unique to specific jobs; for example, a nurse executive is responsible for overseeing the clinical nursing divisions and a CFO is responsible for managing the organization's financial operations. Other functions may be shared by numerous staff members, for example, budgeting and supervisory responsibilities. Knowledgeable individuals must define in detail the required job functions.

As described in the next pages, the importance of adding a section to the position specification that details explicitly the key objectives that the executive needs to achieve in the first year to 15 months can not be emphasized enough. Also, leaders should detail key objectives that might not be fulfilled if the position remains open. Interviewing with these objectives in mind minimizes the possibility that chemistry and fit will distort a good selection decision. Leaders can target candidates who have already achieved the same or similar objectives in other organizations and can ask very specific questions to determine if the individuals have had previous experience achieving specific types of objectives.

Many organizations need help in this area. Requirements are often expressed in ambiguous terms that are difficult or impossible to measure, such as, "requires leadership skills," "requires a candidate who is articulate," "requires strong interpersonal skills," or "prefer candidates who have strong prioritization skills." Considerable confusion can arise about what is *required* and what is *preferred.* For example, is a CPA designation *required* or *preferred* for a CFO position? When a masters degree is *required,* what kind of masters is *preferred?*

The leaders of one organization described a preferred skill for a vice president of marketing simply as "Needs marketing skills." When asked to be more specific, they wrote, "The ideal candidate will be able to evaluate, analyze, and make sense out of mounds of market share and managed care data. He/she will be able to clearly identify and briefly communicate the meaning of these data to individuals such as physicians and board members, who do not have the time or resources to reach such conclusions." Obviously this latter description is much more descriptive and shows that the organization was looking for candidates who could do much more than simply write attractive marketing brochures. Preferred and required qualifications need to be described in explicit detail.

Walter Ulmer, former president of the Center for Creative Leadership in Greensboro, North Carolina, expressed great concern about the lack of definition of critical leadership characteristics. He wrote: "We do a poor job in defining 'successful leaders.' It is possible to be the head of an organization that is doing very well and still be an untrusting despot. Some who have made it to the top of the ladder are 'successful' only in the narrowest sense of the word" (Ulmer 1991).

Develop a position specification, not just a job description

Developing a position specification is much more comprehensive than simply writing a job description. *Job descriptions* are usually lists of generic functions and basic qualifications. *Position specifications* include more detail and greater itemization of how job performance will be measured. They include comprehensive descriptions of attributes, traits, and competencies of the preferred executive or manager.

In his article, "Hiring Without Firing," Claudio Fernandez-Araoz (1999) provides four helpful and guiding questions that those developing a position specification can ask themselves:

1. Two years from now, how are we going to tell whether the new executive has been successful?
2. What is it that we expect him/her to do, and how should he/she go about doing it in our organization?
3. What internal objectives would we agree on?
4. If we were to implement a short- and medium-term incentive system for this position, what key variables would matter most?

Some position specifications contain what are called "critical incidents." Fernandez-Araoz (1999) defines these as "The commonly occurring situations that the new executive will confront and must be able to master to be considered a strong performer." Different than the key objectives that the new person needs to achieve, these situations describe specific circumstances the executive may face. For example, for a CFO, they could be the ability to:

- Handle probing questions by board finance committee members;
- Respond to questions and challenges from line managers without creating the perception of defensiveness or control; and
- Inspire open debate about financial matters.

Appendices 2.1 and 2.2 at the end of this chapter illustrate two sample position specifications. Note the detail described in the "Key Objectives" section. Consider how these objectives can be used later in the interview process to judge the abilities of candidates to achieve such objectives based on prior experience. Note, however, that even in these examples, the required and preferred characteristics could be improved by providing greater specificity as described in the following paragraphs.

Describe attributes and competencies in greater detail

Successful organizations have an uncanny ability to describe preferred characteristics, attributes, and competencies in great detail. Compare the lack of specificity in Organization A's stated qualifications with the level of detail in Organization B's improved list of qualifications.

Organization A: The preferred vice-president candidate will:

- Have strong leadership abilities;
- Demonstrate excellent people skills; and
- Be an excellent communicator.

Organization B: The preferred vice-president candidate will:

- Be a leader who has successfully merged departments of several hospitals during a merger;
- Have had experience working with demanding physicians during stressful times with a merger; and
- Be able to show evidence of successful communications efforts during a merger.

Follow the timetable for the selection process

Organizations most successful in recruiting talent realize the importance of not only setting specific timetables for the process but also in *following* them. A positive signal is sent to candidates when the search progresses as scheduled. Dates for first- and second-round interviews that are established when the search process commences facilitate calendar scheduling for everyone involved. Candidates can be informed of the dates early in the process and asked to hold the dates as they move forward in the interview and selection process. This can save weeks of delay.

CONCLUDING COMMENTS

Much time and effort should go into properly preparing for a leadership search. Most organizations fail when they shortcut this part of the process. Without a search process manager, a clearly delineated plan, and an explicit position specification, organizations will often wander through the executive search and the best decisions will be left more to luck than effective management.

EVALUATE YOUR ORGANIZATION

1. One person is in charge of each leadership search.

Strongly Disagree	Disagree	Neither Disagree or Agree	Agree	Strongly Agree

2. We spend ample time on the front end of the search process determining position needs and key objectives.

Strongly Disagree	Disagree	Neither Disagree or Agree	Agree	Strongly Agree

3. Our searches typically progress at a steady pace.

Strongly Disagree	Disagree	Neither Disagree or Agree	Agree	Strongly Agree

4. Our written descriptions of leadership jobs provide clear specification of needs, key objectives, and required/preferred qualifications.

Strongly Disagree	Disagree	Neither Disagree or Agree	Agree	Strongly Agree

5. We frequently use a position specification document when interviewing candidates.

Strongly Disagree	Disagree	Neither Disagree or Agree	Agree	Strongly Agree

REFERENCES

Fernandez-Araoz, C. 1999. "Hiring Without Firing." *Harvard Business Review* July/August: 115–116.

Gubman, E.L. 1998. *The Talent Solution*. New York: McGraw-Hill, 76.

Hogan, R., and J. Hogan. 1992. *Hogan Personality Inventory Manual,* 2nd ed. Tulsa, OK: Hogan Assessment Systems.

Sorcher, M. *Predicting Executive Success: What It Takes to Make It into Senior Management* (out of print) as quoted in White, R.P., and D.L. DeVries. 1990. "Issues and Observations." *Quarterly Newsletter of the Center for Creative Leadership* 10 (1): 4–5.

Ulmer, W. 1991. "Issues and Observations: Inklings." *Quarterly Newsletter of the Center for Creative Leadership* 10 (1): 7.

White, R.P., and D.L. DeVries. 1990. "Issues and Observations." *Quarterly Newsletter of the Center for Creative Leadership* 10 (1): 6–7.

Sample Position Specification
Health System President/CEO

POSITION FUNCTIONS

The president/CEO reports to the board of trustees and is responsible for the leadership of the entire organization and its various entities. The president and CEO is responsible for the overall leadership of the organization. With accountability to the board, he/she will:

- Develop a vision and mission for the organization that will provide comprehensive health services to the area and region.
- Ensure that the vision and mission is articulated in a meaningful long-range strategic plan that contains measurable goals and objectives.
- Develop annual plans containing measurable objectives that relate to the strategic plan and related issues.
- Oversee the development of monitoring and reporting mechanisms to inform the Board of progress toward the vision and mission of the organization.
- Oversee the development of appropriate budgetary and financial plans to ensure the long-term financial viability of the organization.
- Oversee the development of quality measures to ensure that patients receive the highest quality of care possible and ensure that the organization develops a continuous quality improvement environment.
- Select, develop, and lead a senior management team to oversee the overall operations of the organization and its various business units and entities.

- Develop and maintain strong collegial working relationships with physicians.
- Develop and maintain an environment that allows employees to maximize their involvement and service within the organization.
- Actively relate to various individuals and groups within the community to ensure that the organization is viewed as a good neighbor and that it exercises the appropriate leadership within community affairs.
- Engage in appropriate corporate and personal behavior in serving as a positive role model for the organization and the community.

KEY OBJECTIVES

The candidate must achieve the following goals and objectives to be successful within the first 12 to 18 months.

- Complete the merger. While many aspects of the merger have gone smoothly, the separate component parts (organizational entities) continue to indicate that the organization has not yet fully developed its new identity and culture. There are still some who say, "We are Hospital A" or "We are Hospital B." The new president and CEO will need to help various stakeholders understand how to successfully integrate within an effective health system. He/she will make steady progress in developing and advancing a new culture.
- Graciously acknowledge the gifts of various benefactors and enlist the help of these supporters in sustaining the newly developed vision. The new president and CEO also must develop and implement an organizationwide strategy covering the use of gifts to achieve organizational objectives.

- Build unity and a commitment to the organization's vision among board members, medical staff, employees, and other stakeholders.
- Help to further develop the board through the visioning process. The board and senior leadership engage in this process to better determine what programs and services they will offer, their geographic service areas, organizations they might acquire, joint ventures they might engage in, among many other things. A visioning process starts with a fairly simple statement of "what we would like to become" and then guides the leadership through a process to determine how to move in that direction.
- Develop a focused and compelling vision. The new president and CEO must work collaboratively with senior leaders and board members to develop this vision and ensure that the organization begins to move aggressively in this direction. The president and CEO must be able to see the disparate elements and champion a better way of developing a common culture and organization. The vision must include a plan that encompasses all constituencies and addresses how the tertiary services that cover a large geographic area should blend with other locally based and oriented patient care services.
- Communicate the new vision and culture within the organization and beyond to the community in a simple, pragmatic, and understandable manner.
- Assess the financial performance of the organization and develop specific strategies to ensure long-term strength. Ensure effective management of the organization's operations.
- Develop a "physician partnering" environment. The new president and CEO must ensure that physicians feel represented and understood.
- Increase strength of relationships with the community.

SKILLS AND COMPETENCIES

The ideal candidate will possess the following characteristics, skills, experience, and competencies (not in priority order).

- A recognized track record of success in developing health systems and leading complex organizations. The candidate should understand how component system parts best fit together, how cultures are merged, and how to develop a unified vision within a well-integrated health system.
- Progressive leadership experience in a variety of healthcare organizations. Ideally, experience should include leadership in an organization with tertiary components and other recognized centers of excellence.
- Strong financial and operational acumen and an understanding of the essential elements of a well-managed organization.
- Ability to build and retain a strong management team and an outlook that welcomes challenges.
- An exceptional work ethic and ability to work long hours to achieve significant results. The candidate will be comfortable translating vision and goals into specific measurable events and enjoy being held accountable for achieving specific measurable results.
- Ability to develop trust relationships with individuals and groups and to quickly bring disparate groups together. The successful president and CEO also will have the ability to ensure the continued participation of those who do not fully join consensus views.
- Significant experience working with boards and a demonstrated ability to communicate effectively with them.
- Ability to work collaboratively and in close partnership with physicians.
- An open, approachable, and decisive style. This executive style is key to effective decision making and to relationships

with physicians, employees, and other stakeholders.

- High visibility within the community and sensitivity to the various issues existing between the community and the organization.
- Experience with and a high interest in participating in fundraising and philanthropic events and programs.
- A strong internal moral compass and ability to serve as a personal and professional role model for others.
- A high comfort level in working with a strong team of senior executives and a track record of building strong leadership teams.

An M.H.A. or other advanced degree strongly preferred.

Sample Position Specification
Health System Vice President
Medical Affairs

GENERAL RESPONSIBILITIES

The vice president provides leadership, direction, and administration of the medical operations for systemwide activities and entities. He/she is responsible for quality oversight, coordination within the medical staff, the recruitment of additional physicians, working with senior management in business plan development, marketing and public relations, budget analysis, and cost-effectiveness. The vice president will ensure compliance with established objectives and the realization of quality and economical health management services.

In addition to traditional physician leadership activity within the system's hospital, the vice president also will serve two other functions. First, he or she will be the northern region liaison with the physician corporation for the parent health system. Second, he or she will serve as the chief medical officer for the system's home healthcare and long-term-care entities.

The vice president will be provided an opportunity for some limited clinical work, depending on his or her specialty. For example, arrangements may be made for the physician vice president to interact clinically within the system in occupational medicine, second coverage in the emergency department, or urgent care.

Accountable To: CEO

Accountable For: Physician recruitment, medical staff relations, infection control, medical staff quality improvement, risk management, utilization review, medical staff coordination, social work, MSO, PHO, medical staff leadership, medical staff development/integration, and quality improvement.

JOB ROLES / ACCOUNTABILITIES

Management/Operations Functions

- Directs activities of assigned departments/areas of responsibility in accordance with system's guiding principles, policies and objectives.
- Oversees and manages the medical staff services including credentialing, corrective actions, hospital quality and professional care appraisal, mandatory consultation, and any other process required by medical staff bylaws.
- Ensures compliance with all regulatory agencies governing delivery of health management services and rules of accrediting bodies by continuously monitoring the system's medical operations and programs and initiating changes where required.
- Establishes short and long-term operating objectives in accordance with the system's overall strategic plans and program.
- Provides administrative support to the MSO and PHO.
- Assesses and evaluates present and future needs, trends, problems, and opportunities.
- Applies the knowledge and skills necessary to provide care appropriate to the age of the patients/clients served (i.e., infant, pediatric, adolescent, adult, and geriatric).
- Maintains established department policies, procedures, objectives, quality assurance programs, and safety standards.

Process Improvement Functions

- Works collaboratively as part of senior leadership in strategic plan development and implementation.

- Works with the appropriate hospital staff in program development, including business plan development, physician recruiting, quality improvement, and cost-effectiveness.
- Develops and maintains an environment characterized by a high level of medical staff involvement in quality, patient satisfaction, medical management, and utilization review.
- Actively supports and participates in process improvement efforts and in team functions/decisions.
- Directs a systematic approach to continuous improvement through the use of quality tools and management principles. Ensures continuous assessment and improvement.

Customer Service Functions

- Works collaboratively with all hospital levels and business units.
- Represents the system and its entities in fostering positive relationships with other health agencies, organizations, groups, government agencies, third-party payers, and the community.
- Serves as a role model for consistent demonstration of and advocacy for hospital's guiding principles.
- Demonstrates knowledge about and respect for patient, service provider, and organizational confidentiality procedures and protocols.
- Maintains and protects patients' rights.

Personal Development Functions

- Maintains and proves personal and professional learning and development through literature, seminars, workshops, and affiliations.
- Learns new skills/competencies and maintains current competencies through education programs, inservices, and meetings.

KEY GOALS

Because this is a newly created position and represents the first time the hospital will have a medical officer, the most obvious primary first-year goals is the development of the position's role. Other initial expectations and goals include the following:

- *Quality improvement.* The new vice president will lead the quality "journey" for the hospital and help move the organization to the next level of quality improvement across the continuum of care.
- *Physician alignment.* The vice president will help to develop and sustain an environment in which the medical staffs of the system's hospitals are linked cohesively to the community.
- *Alignment within the region and parent health system corporation.* The new vice president will help lead the hospital physician collective as it more closely links with the total parent health system region.
- *Physician recruitment and PHO/MSO leadership.* The vice president will work directly with hospital physicians, hospital senior leadership and board, and parent health system senior leadership to recruit necessary physicians and to enhance PHO and MSO operations.

JOB QUALIFICATIONS

The likely candidate will be an individual with prior administrative healthcare experience and clearly demonstrated leadership qualities. He/she will understand trends in healthcare delivery systems, managed care, and community care. Additionally, the preferred candidate will have working experience in the merger of healthcare organizations. Preferred candidates may be in the number two leadership position in larger systems, vice presidents of medical administration in smaller systems, or individuals with unique combinations of leadership roles and responsibilities. The individual must understand primary care practice, physician accountability, and physician alignment. He/she must be sensitive to the needs of both employed and private practitioners and be able to forge consensus in the physician collective.

EDUCATION, LICENSURE, AND CERTIFICATION

- MD or DO required.
- Current state licensure as physician.
- Board certified and eligible for full medical staff privileges.
- BA, MHA, MPH or related graduate degree preferred.

COMPETENCIES, SKILLS, AND ABILITIES

- Possesses ability to grasp and lead systems.
- Understands the variability of work in planning and problem solving.
- Understands how people learn, develop, and improve and why they behave as they do.
- Understands the interaction between and interdependence of systems, variability, learning, and human behavior.
- Possesses ability to give the organization vision, meaning, direction, and focus.
- Deals effectively with a changing environment and is open to new ideas.
- Possesses knowledge about medical staff working practices.
- Possesses knowlede about financial and human resources issues, including budgeting, financial forecasting, patient care financing, managed care, capitation, and conflict management and intervention.
- Possesses excellent meeting management and presentation skills.

- Analyzes and understands statistical data, benchmarking data, and conceptual information.
- Demonstrates sound clinical skills and judgment.
- Possesses excellent human relations and oral/written communications skills.
- Manages conflict, builds consensus, and negotiates effectively.
- Demonstrates interest in and ability to work in an interdisciplinary environment.

CHAPTER 3

Sourcing to Find Superior Talent

"The real key to getting the best leadership talent is knowing where to find it—knowing how to look for it, understanding the best places to look, and uncovering talented
managers and executives who are not looking for work.
Getting the best involves extra effort in seeking out people
on a broader scale and getting the word out as widely as
possible."

—*A long-time executive search consultant*

ONCE THE NEED for a leadership position is well defined,
the next critical step is *finding* the talent to meet those needs to
fill the available job. In the executive search industry, this step is
called *sourcing* because it involves calling or contacting multiple
"sources" to obtain candidate referrals. Sourcing includes all activities related to getting the word out about an opportunity, selling
the job, community, and organization, and getting qualified people interested in the opportunity. In many respects, sourcing is
marketing—a reality that, unfortunately, many healthcare organizations fail to fully realize.

Healthcare organizations traditionally have used a number of
approaches to finding leadership talent. These include running
advertisements and, more recently, posting the position on the
Internet; using human resources executives to contact potential

candidates; and engaging the services of a search firm. A brief description of each follows.

Advertising

Many organizations believe that running advertisements for their open leadership positions, either in newspapers or professional journals, is the only approach required for sourcing. Ads fall short, however, for several reasons.

- *Ads are very expensive.* A single, two-column ad in a major Sunday newspaper can cost up to $5,000. To attract the attention of candidates in several cities, the organization may need to purchase ads in as many as five or six newspapers.
- *Ads require extensive lead time and response is slow.* Running ads in journals may require as much as seven to eight weeks of lead time. Beyond this time period, an organization may actually wait as long as two months or more before receiving any response from the ads.
- *Ads may not be noted by top leadership talent.* Running ads assumes that the talent an organization wishes to attract actually will see, read, and respond to the ad. Busy and successful leaders may miss a newspaper ad altogether, or worse yet, live in a city where the ad is not run. Moreover, they may not see journal ads or not see them in time to respond. Finally, some individuals simply do not read or respond to ads.
- *Ads are space-limited.* There is seldom enough room in the typical ad to adequately represent the opportunity. Short of paying for a cost-prohibitive, full-page ad, it is practically impossible to capture the full essence of the need and the opportunity. Additionally, unlike direct telephone calls to discuss position openings, ads are not interactive.
- *Ads are not targeted.* They are famous (or infamous) for generating hundreds of nonqualified responses. Organization

staff responding to the volume of phone calls, emails, and letter/resumés from nonqualified candidates could better spend their time dealing with more qualified individuals.

- *Ads are not productive.* According to one industry expert, individuals responding to ads fill fewer than 15 percent of all leadership jobs in all industries (Jones 2001).

Internet postings

Some healthcare organizations have begun to explore the use of the Internet for job postings. Yet according to Russ Jones (2001), very few leadership positions in healthcare are handled today through the Internet (technical position postings are more common). It also is important to note that the Internet approach generates many of the same problems as the newspaper or journal ad approach. While this likely will change during the next decade, the Internet currently is not an effective or targeted approach to finding healthcare leadership talent.

A review of some of the more popular web sites that focus on recruitment, such as www.headhunter.net (which has a healthcare section), www.healthjobs-usa.com, www.speedyresume.com (which has a management category), www.careermag.com, or www.hire-health.com, will enlighten readers by showing the difficulty of reviewing thousands of online resumés and the small exposure given to higher level management jobs. Perhaps the most targeted web site for healthcare leadership recruiting and postings is the American College of Healthcare Executives (ACHE) web site, www.ache.org/career.html.

Human resource staff

Some healthcare organizations use their human resource staff to source or find leadership talent. The staff may use traditional search firm techniques, such as direct telephone calls to individuals in the same or similar positions, or direct mail letters or emails to potential candidates. In most organizations today, however, human resource executives are exceedingly busy. Sourcing is not their primary job; they simply cannot give it the time it deserves or requires. Also, few have the research capability or membership lists to develop comprehensive slates of potential candidates.

Search firms

Finally, many healthcare organizations today are turning to search firms for help with sourcing. Having experienced many of the problems with ads and other approaches described above, organizations frequently find that search firms can at least provide greater access to a larger number of qualified candidates. Chapter 9 is devoted to the topic of the use of search firms in finding healthcare executive talent.

Enhancing Sourcing

By identifying and attracting candidates, sourcing provides the "life blood" of the executive recruitment process. It includes the following components:

- *Finding talent:* knowing how and where to reach candidates;
- *Attracting talent:* knowing how to sell these candidates on the benefits of considering the opportunity; and
- *Screening talent:* knowing which candidates merit additional discussion and review (not as comprehensive as evaluating talent).

A description of each follows.

Finding leadership talent seems like it should be a simple task. Yet at the leadership level, it can be quite daunting. Organizations handling searches on their own need to make sourcing calls. Often the problem is not knowing who to call or write. Finding talent is in many respects simply getting the word out. There are many simple ways that healthcare organizations can attack this challenge, including sending personalized letters (see figure 3.1) announcing the job opening to:

- CEOs and other senior executives of other organizations;
- Executives of state and local hospital associations;
- Members of health administration program alumni lists;
- Graduate health administration program directors;
- Healthcare consultants;
- Healthcare attorneys;
- Healthcare audit partners; and
- Attendees of relevant seminars and conventions.

Several guides, such as *The Blue Book* and the *HCIA Guide to the Health Care Industry,* list specific executives and managers in healthcare organization. The American Hospital Association *Annual Guide Issue* provides the names of CEOs. If proprietary lists are used, the organization should ensure that usage is approved by the list owner.

When sending the letter, it is wise to include a complete description of the job, the organization, and the community. Some organizations include an extra copy of the document so that it can be easily passed on to others. An extensive written position specification, including details about the organization and the community (see chapter 2) can be a very helpful marketing tool to attract talent and sell the job and the organization.

Figure 3.1 Sample "Get the Word Out" Letter

Dear Colleague:

ABC Health System is seeking a strong patient relations executive. Our vice president of patient relations is retiring after 15 years in the job. Our organization has had several consecutive years of profitability, is known by physicians in our community for being very physician-friendly, and our nursing vacancy rate is under 7 percent.

The ideal candidate presently is in an executive role in nursing leadership. He or she also has had experience leading other clinical departments such as pathology, radiology, and pharmacy. The ideal person will enjoy working with a team that works by consensus and shares in organizational achievements.

A compensation and benefits package that is in the 75th percentile of the market will be provided.

I would appreciate your suggestions of candidates. Please have them contact me directly at 222-222-2222 or by e-mail at recruiter@ abchealth.org.

E-mail also provides a vehicle to get the word out. Because e-mails tend to be shorter than letters, people often are more responsive because they feel they can provide a short reply. Many membership lists, which can be obtained by members or member organizations or purchased, include e-mail addresses. The organization's open leadership position can also be posted on the organization's web site.

Although letters or e-mails can get the word out quickly to a large number of people, targeted telephone calls may be the best method of sourcing. Being able to describe the position verbally and respond to questions on the spot often proves effective. Typically, in most healthcare organizations, the chief human resources officer makes sourcing and recruitment calls. This individual can be very effective if he or she allocates the time and resources needed to gather names and phone numbers of potential candidates. Obviously, due to other responsibilities, this person cannot make calls on a full-time basis, which is why organizations often turn to a search firm.

Name-gathering calls from CEOs can be very effective. In one organization, a new CEO who had just moved to a hospital in a new state had a CFO opening. He called the head of the state hospital association and asked this individual to identify the top ten CFOs in the state. The CEO personally called each individual, describing the CFO opportunity. He invited three to interview with him for the position, and ultimately hired one. Some CEOs call certain colleagues and ask them for suggestions of candidates. Others call people who have attended relevant conferences they themselves attended. Finally, some join a group, such as The Healthcare Roundtable, and contact group peer members for suggestions.

Another innovative approach used by several consulting and auditing firms, most notably McKinsey & Company, is to develop an "alumni club." Club members include anyone who moves on to other jobs and other companies, considered in McKinsey & Company's case, "McKinsey graduates." The organization keeps in close contact with these graduates, often contacting them for information or referrals.

Attracting talent

As described fully in chapter 1, prior to attracting talent, an organization must examine and determine what prospective leaders might wish to find in an organization. This involves a thorough evaluation of all aspects of the culture, the job, the leadership team, and the opportunity. But it also involves creating some method to communicate the organization's positive attributes. For the purposes of this chapter, attracting talent means knowing how to sell prospective candidates on the benefits of considering the opportunity.

How might a healthcare organization promote, publicize, and present the "magnet" factors of its culture? Through marketing in its purest sense, the organization may want to provide written literature detailing the successes of the organization and how executives and managers are involved in these successes. Giving seminars on the organization's best practices at ACHE and other national or regional meetings is another way to market. Organizations may want to compile a package of their best public relations literature and send it to potential candidates. Included could be a "key facts and statistics" sheet that describes the organization and its key indicators. Annual reports also can be very helpful in telling the organization's "story."

Getting the word out can also be accomplished by active networking, membership in organizations such as The Healthcare Roundtable, or authoring articles. Over time, the organization and its leadership team develop quality reputations, which in turn helps recruitment of leadership talent. The bottom line in attracting high-quality talent is to think a little more creatively about how to portray and communicate the organization's positive characteristics.

Screening talent

After an organization has identified and attracted talent through the acquisition of resumés or curriculum vitae, the next step is to screen the candidates against the job requirements. The goal is to identify the candidates who merit additional discussion and review.

Preliminary screening assumes many shapes and forms. Most initial screening takes place through telephone discussions. The conversations typically involve a back-and-forth exchange of information. The organization's representative asks questions to learn more about the candidate and the candidate asks questions to learn more about the position. The most appropriate staff person to make the majority of these calls is an executive-level leader. The person making the call should be at least at the same level as the person who is being called. This ensures that numerous questions can be answered on the spot and increases the likelihood that the person being called will be curious to know more about the job.

Those doing the screening, whether human resources staff, other executives, or search consultants, must be prepared to make the most of each call. Obviously, this means getting enough additional information about the candidate to determine if a face-to-face interview is warranted and should be scheduled. However, it also means being prepared to answer the prospective candidate's questions. Individuals may ask detailed questions about why the position is vacant, what happened to the incumbent, and the compensation level. Poor responses or no response at all may discourage very promising candidates. When sourcing, those making the calls must understand that not everyone is ready and willing to change jobs, even if they have sent a resumé. They must be "sold" on the opportunity.

Typical telephone screening includes the following:

- *Determining genuine interest.* Some candidates really are just "kicking the tires" and do not have a sincere interest in the job. Others may take an active role in initial discussions solely for the purpose of doing their own market survey of compensation. Interviewers can ask, Now that you know a little about this vacancy and the organization, can you tell me why you might be interested in the position? or Why might you want to make a move now?
- *Evaluating enthusiasm and fit.* These are very difficult tasks and often cannot be accomplished over the telephone. Yet preliminary phone screening frequently includes some questions to evaluate fit, such as, Tell me how you deal with conflict during a team meeting? Can you briefly describe your leadership style? or What would your boss tell me about your ability to get along with others on the senior team?
- *Gathering additional facts to clarify the resumé.* With the current trend for abbreviated two-page resumés, organizations often need to obtain a significant amount of additional information.

- *Determining commonality and shared commitment to vision and mission.* When two people talk for the first time, they tend to spend much of the time finding out about each other's goals and values. Questions can be asked such as, What makes you want to get back into a teaching hospital? You have spent most of your career in pediatric hospitals. Why do you seek this position in an adult hospital? You have not yet worked in a faith-based organization. What are your concerns about doing so?
- *Further presenting the job, the organization, and the community.* The organization's representative answers questions and engages in a marketing effort.
- *Determining the next steps with the candidate.* These might include scheduling a face-to-face interview, mutually ending the contact, or some variation in between.

Other approaches to screening include hurdle and holistic screening. *Hurdle screening* entails screening all candidates according to specific requirements that have been carefully identified. Candidates that do not meet the hurdle requirements are eliminated. *Holistic screening* involves identifying and simultaneously weighing positive characteristics of each candidate with specific requirements.

For example, a healthcare organization might state that candidates for the CFO position *must* be CPAs. The CPA requirement is a *hurdle* requirement. All candidates who lack CPA certification are eliminated from consideration. An organization using *holistic* screening might state that it strongly prefers to have candidates with experience in bond financing and managing primary care capitation financial reimbursement. Candidates who do not have experience in these two areas may still be considered if they have other positive characteristics, such as working for a similar organization or strong recommendations.

In the ideal world, healthcare organization staff should both screen and respond to all resumés and expressions of interest. Screening based on the hurdle method can quickly eliminate many candidates who are not at all qualified. Letters should be sent to these candidates as soon as possible to reduce the amount of time that may be spent later responding to them. Figure 3.2 offers a sample "no thank you" letter.

Finally, like many other aspects of talent management, screening can be improved by simply adopting a more formal process and approach. Using a blueprint for the preliminary screening process can save valuable time, avoid potential embarrassments later, and greatly enhance the chance of finding the most suitable candidate. A brief sample blueprint appears in Figure 3.3.

Highly effective organizations use a *structured* process to review resumés. Before the first person is brought to the organization for face-to-face interviews, the organization follows a process or methodology to review resumés and determine who might best meet the requirements of the job. Elements of the structured process include:

- *Screen resumés.* Ideally, the resumés received provide information that enables the reviewer to match candidates' specific past accomplishments with required objectives for the new leader. When resumés do not facilitate such review, some search consultants and employers actually return the resumés to the candidates asking them to redesign them with more specific emphasis on achievements.

Figure 3.2 Sample "No Thank You" Letter to Prospective Candidates

Dear Candidate:

Thank you very much for your response to our ad for a chief financial officer. Although your experience and credentials appear strong, we have narrowed our consideration list to only those candidates who have the CPA certification. For a variety of reasons, we feel that CPA certification is one key to success for our new CFO in the current healthcare environment.

We do wish you continuing success in your career.

Figure 3.3 Sample Screening Blueprint

Job Requirements:
CPA   Yes _____   No _____
MBA   Yes _____   No _____
Five or more years experience   Yes _____   No _____
Specific experience in issuing bonds   Yes _____   No _____

- *Review resumés with a focus on making a match.* A match is identified when the needs of the job parallel the specific achievements outlined by the candidates. In essence, in finding strong talent, the past is often a very good predictor of the future. For example, if one of the key objectives for a CFO position is to reduce days in accounts receivable (AR), the resumés of candidates who have a highlighted AR reduction as an accomplishment will get selected for further review.
- *Conduct telephone screening.* To reduce candidate travel expense and enhance the quality of the resumé review, a telephone screen may be warranted. Top candidates as determined from the resumé review are called and asked specific, targeted questions focused on the required job objectives. Those making the calls should remember that the telephone screen provides an opportunity to sell the organization and the community.

CONCLUDING COMMENTS

Traditional methods of finding candidates such as newspaper or journal advertising will not work effectively during times of leadership talent wars. Organizations need to discover other more creative methods. They also need to exercise more productive screening methods to enhance the effectiveness of evaluating candidates early in the search process.

EVALUATE YOUR ORGANIZATION

1. Our organization uses multiple methods of finding management and executive candidates.

Strongly Disagree	Disagree	Neither Disagree or Agree	Agree	Strongly Agree

2. Our organization has the reputation and enough visibility in our hospital or other healthcare association to attract leadership talent.

Strongly Disagree	Disagree	Neither Disagree or Agree	Agree	Strongly Agree

3. Our organization achieves visibility in the industry through presentations by our leaders at state and local healthcare associations, articles published in the professional literature, and other means.

Strongly Disagree	Disagree	Neither Disagree or Agree	Agree	Strongly Agree

4. Preliminary screening of candidates by telephone is done methodically and by competent senior individuals.

Strongly Disagree	Disagree	Neither Disagree or Agree	Agree	Strongly Agree

5. Our organization acknowledges all expressions of interest in employment for leadership positions.

Strongly Disagree	Disagree	Neither Disagree or Agree	Agree	Strongly Agree

REFERENCE

Jones, R. 2001. National outplacement consultant with First Transitions. Personal communication, April.

CHAPTER 4

Interviewing and Evaluation

"There is probably no more important management function than interviewing candidates for executive positions— but although we all know and recognize this, we don't properly prepare for it and we often foul it up."

—*A health system CEO*

THE QUOTE ABOVE suggests that many organizations could and should do a better job in the interview and evaluation part of the selection process. The personal interview is *the* vehicle where selection decisions are made. However, face-to-face interviews are often the most subjective aspect of the talent management process. As mentioned in chapter 2, a selection decision needs to be much more than just a gut-feel. The chemistry or fit must be well defined. Leadership selection is one of the most important decisions any organization will face, yet few organizations prepare and apply themselves as they should in making these important decisions.

Often the problem is the lack of organizational focus and intensity on the actual interview and evaluation process. Competing issues interfere. Busy leaders, faced with other items on their to-do lists, are barraged by telephone calls, e-mails, and meetings. Often, it is difficult for them to set aside time to prepare for the interview. Instead, they put it off until the candidate arrives. Poorly prepared, leaders allow the interview to become an unstructured conversation.

IMPROVING THE INTERVIEW AND EVALUATION PROCESS

If adhered to closely, the following strategies will help ensure a more comprehensive and effective interview and evaluation process.

Increase prescreening

Front-end prescreening, both in terms of quantity and quality, should be increased prior to arranging in-person interviews. Few organizations commit the required time to this and often find themselves frustrated with the lack of quality candidates. Inadequate telephone screening increases the chances that poorly qualified candidates will appear for in-person interviews. To narrow the selection choices, consider using a questionnaire that asks for a more detailed description of experiences and accomplishments (see chapter 3).

Define in detail the purpose of the interview

One critical question for the interviewing process is remarkably simple. It is, What is the interview designed to accomplish? Consider the following options:

- It is designed to elicit additional information;
- It is designed to verify details about past experiences;
- It is designed to evaluate interpersonal style and fit; or

- It is designed to provide additional information about the leadership vacancy.

Most interviews turn into conversations that focus almost exclusively on fit and interpersonal issues.

One eastern health system CEO, well known for his comprehensive approach to executive interviews, made it a practice to open all interviews with candidates by describing the interview process and indicating the tasks assigned to each person on the day's interviewing roster. He shared his end goals for the interview process, and in essence, provided a road map for the day. Candidates emerged from the initial interview with the CEO with an excellent feel for the structure of the interview process.

Determine the interview team and respective roles

Determining who will be involved in interviewing candidates is a difficult process. Often, political agendas rather than logic dictate who is "in" on the process. The higher the position, the larger the interview team will be. Hence, a team interviewing CEO candidates will be the largest and broadest. As many board members as possible should be included, as should a broad and representative grouping of the medical staff. Because of the effect a CEO can have in and on the community, some healthcare organizations include on the interviewing team community leaders who are not board members.

The team interviewing candidates for an open senior executive position should include all peer executives, selected board and medical staff members, and managers to be supervised by the executive. It generally is best *not* to ask those to be supervised by the executive to complete executive interview evaluations. Their input might create discomfort later if a person of whom they were critical were to become their boss.

Teams interviewing physician executive leadership candidates should include a large cross section of the medical staff leadership, for example, representatives of the medical executive committee, department chairs, and other informal leaders.

Beyond who will be on the team, more thought must be given to the interview role to be assumed by each individual. Successful organizations do the following.

- *Predetermine who asks which questions.* Do not allow this part of the selection process to be done haphazardly. Assign specific questions to each participant in the process, as appropriate to their responsibilities. For example, the human resources executive would ask specific questions about how the candidates dealt with difficult people problems. The CFO would ask candidates to describe in detail their budgeting experience.
- *Assign certain questions to all interviewers.* For example, all might ask, How have you fit into teams such as ours in the past? Or, Describe in some detail your method for selling new ideas to a leadership team. Variation in responses can shed light on the candidate's experience and comfort level with team participation.
- *Assign selected interviewers a specific role in providing basic information.* For example, the human resources executive might be assigned the duty of describing the benefits package while another executive might be asked to talk about the choice of school systems and real estate in the community. Similarly, a long-time executive might be asked to provide a brief history of the organization.

Train the interviewers

Even the most seasoned executives often need training in interviewing. Training provides interviewers with a detailed understanding of the legal aspects of interviewing, how to craft targeted questions that elicit required facts, and how to ask follow-up questions. There is little doubt that training can improve the quality of the ultimate hiring decision. However, training must be performed by an individual with experience with executive hiring decisions. Often a search consultant is the best person to handle this task for a senior executive team.

Ensure that proper time is allotted for interviews

Adequate time must be allocated for interviews. Honoring the interview time schedule is also important. Delaying candidates in the waiting room to place last minute telephone calls or to take a quick (or first!) look at resumés is not only impolite but can turn off highly qualified candidates.

To allow more people to participate in the interview process, some organizations shorten the interview time to 30 minutes. This is not ample time to get to know candidates, their background, and their style. A minimum of 60 minutes should be allocated for each interview. Additional time for interviews involving direct reports is critical. Senior leaders interviewing an executive-level person who will report to them should spend no less than four to six hours interviewing top candidates. Allocating the hours over two different time periods often proves beneficial.

For example, a CEO interviewing a CFO candidate might conduct the first interview in the first week of October, and then bring back the candidate in a week or two for a follow-up session. The nature of the two interviews differs significantly. During the first interview, the CEO gathers facts and asks basic questions, such as, Have you ever done X or Y? Where did you work when you did this? What were the results? During the follow-up interview, the CEO gathers additional specifics and begins more personal discussions about style and fit.

Ask the tough questions

As long as they are legal, not designed to discriminate, and directly related to the job, tough questions can and should be asked during the interview. Questions such as the chronology of job history or why the individual left his or her last job should be asked as early in the process as possible.

As a general legal rule of thumb, no question should be asked that elicits "protected" information about a candidate who is in a "protected class category." Because individuals cannot be discriminated against based on race, color, creed, sex, national origin, handicap status, or age (40 and over), questions that address these matters with individuals in a protected class should not be asked.

Another general legal rule of thumb is to ask only questions that are directly related to the job itself. Questions about age, marital status, and similar matters are not pertinent to the ability to do a job and thus should not be asked.

Asking tough questions is less related to the specifics of the question and more related to the ability of the interviewer to probe deeper. A snorkel-versus-scuba-dive analogy might help clarify the distinction. The interviewer who scuba dives asks follow-up questions that relate to the earlier questions. These deeper questions seek additional clarification and amplification. The interviewer who snorkels asks a single question, listens for the answer, and then moves forward with the next question rather than probing and exploring a greater depth of response.

Most interviewers are afraid of asking detailed questions. Or, they avoid the often uncomfortable feelings that can arise during a frank discussion by simply deciding, "I will not hire this person." Candid and direct discussions that raise conflict are uncomfortable for many people. Almost everyone needs better training in having direct, open, and forthright conversations. Interviews are a great place to begin.

For example, during one selection process, a candidate was scheduled for a full day of interviews. He began the morning with the CEO who was known for his ability to be direct and honest. During that interview, the CEO and candidate conversed openly and reached the conclusion that it did not make sense for the candidate to continue the interview process because his qualifications and experience did not meet the needs of the job. The candidate left with a very positive impression of the CEO and was able to return home on an earlier flight. The other executives on the interview team were able to spend the time previously scheduled for interviews more productively.

Develop and use a written evaluation tool

A written evaluation tool—filled out by each interviewer to summarize the candidate's skills, qualifications, and experience as communicated by the interviewee—helps interviewers recall and categorize the candidate's major strengths and weaknesses. When interviewers review the tool prior to conducting the interview, they have a better feel for the depth of information they should obtain during the interview process. Many organizations still do not use such a tool, relying instead on interviewers' random notes and recall. Two sample evaluation tools appear as Appendices 4.1 and 4.2 at the end of the chapter. The information requested for Appendix 4.2, tied directly to the requirements in the position specification, is likely to prove even more helpful than those for Appendix 4.1, which is a generic leadership assessment questionnaire.

Create rules to minimize evaluation bias during the interview process

There should be no discussion of the candidates until (1) all executives have interviewed them, and (2) all written evaluation sheets have been turned in. Consider the following example that illustrates why these rules should be observed.

A candidate for a professional services vice-president position begins the interview process with a breakfast interview with the CFO. During the interview, the CFO and the candidate discover that they grew up in the same area of the country and have several acquaintances in common. Following the positive and spirited interview, the CFO goes to a budget meeting with two other executives who will later interview the candidate. These executives ask the CFO about his impressions of the candidate. If the CFO enjoys a good working relationship with his two executive colleagues, an upbeat report on the candidate by the CFO obviously will increase the probability that the executives will begin their interviews with the candidate with a positive bias. Conversely, a negative bias could be created by the CFO if the CFO didn't like the candidate (perhaps the candidate arrived late the night before, did not get ample rest, was not exceptionally sharp in the first interview, and did not have anything in common with the CFO).

Some organizations like to bring the entire interviewing team together to discuss all candidates after all the interviews are completed. Although this can be a successful approach, it has some dangers. These include ignoring the actual results of the written evaluation sheets, allowing some of the team members to more strongly influence the selection than others, or lack of forthcomingness and candid opinions from the more reserved members of the group who wait to see how the CEO or their boss feels before offering their thoughts.

Manage the interview process

Simple rules can make the interview process run smoothly. They include:

- Show respect for the process.
- Stay on time.

- Ensure that administrative assistants know the importance of the interviews and do not interrupt with telephone calls or questions.
- Respect the personal needs of candidates by providing restroom breaks, water, and meals.

Use second, follow-up interviews

Popular wisdom today usually dictates the use of a second interview. Second interviews provide an excellent opportunity for more targeted questions and a chance for the spouse to see the community. Specific details should be worked out by both parties regarding job expectations, responsibilities, and concerns. When occurring after targeted reference checking, second interviews also provide an opportunity to deal with any concerns about a candidate. They should be carefully planned to ensure that lingering questions about capability, style, qualifications, or interpersonal matters are addressed.

Consider using psychological tests and work-ups

To assist in the evaluation of final candidates, an increasing number of organizations are using psychological tests or work-ups performed by licensed psychologists. Caution should be exercised in this regard. Because of the importance of this topic, chapter 10 addresses it in detail.

Take care of the candidate

Organizations often overlook the fact that interviewing is a two-way street or "dating" exercise. They need to recognize and take care of the "other side" of the interview. Many recruitment efforts fail solely because the organization ignores this angle of talent management. Basics of taking good care of candidates include the following.

- Provide extensive and informative literature about the organization and the community. Organizations should prepare attractive and wide-ranging information packages and provide them to candidates *before* the first interview. Included could be organizational statistics and charts, strategic plan summaries, details about the position and its responsibilities, benefits and retirement information, incentive compensation plans and how bonuses are earned, area real estate information including a copy of a recent multiple listings book, school and local information available from the chamber of commerce, and other information that would give the candidate a better feel for the organization and its community.
- Provide information about the organization's financial condition during the first round of interviews. Many organizations prefer to wait until the end of the interview process; yet, some candidates may actually withdraw from the process or choose to never enter it due to concern about the unspoken.
- Recruit the whole family, not just the candidate. This may include the need to fly the children to the location as well as the spouse.
- Make the visit more comfortable and hospitable by doing those "little things," such as meeting the candidate and family at the airport, choosing an appropriate hotel, ensuring a welcome basket and flowers in the hotel room, or providing a companion for the children by pairing them during excursions or activities with executives' children of similar ages and interests.

Taking care of the candidate requires a firm understanding and buy-in to the essential goals of the interview process. Interviews must be focused and applicable conversations centered around data gathering, mutual exchange of information, and the exploration of mutual expectations. Interviews also must provide the opportunity for mutual assessment and selling of the position, the organization, the leadership team, and the community.

CONCLUDING COMMENTS

Interviews must be designed and conducted to minimize the natural biases that occur during the interview process. How can this be done? Organizations should (Heneman et al. 1989):

- Train the interviewers.
- Develop questions based on job analysis.
- Dedicate more time to interviews.
- Consistently administer the process to all applicants. Ask the same questions of each applicant (that is, structure the interview.)
- Train those interviewing to focus vigorously on asking deeper follow-up questions, especially when they hear a comment that causes concern.
- Be certain that the interview process is designed carefully to minimize comments that can bias ultimate results.
- Develop rating scales for evaluating applicants, and anchor the scales for scoring answers with examples and illustrations.
- Have an interview panel conduct the interviews, record answers, and rate the applicants.

These efforts will help ensure that the interview process uncovers or reveals the very best possible leadership talent.

EVALUATE YOUR ORGANIZATION

1. The interview process in our organization is carefully thought-out.

Strongly Disagree	Disagree	Neither Disagree or Agree	Agree	Strongly Agree

2. Our organization has a formal process to evaluate candidates during on-site interviews.

Strongly Disagree	Disagree	Neither Disagree or Agree	Agree	Strongly Agree

3. The role of each person assigned to interview candidates is carefully defined and scripted.

Strongly Disagree	Disagree	Neither Disagree or Agree	Agree	Strongly Agree

4. A written evaluation sheet is used by interviewers following interviews.

Strongly Disagree	Disagree	Neither Disagree or Agree	Agree	Strongly Agree

5. Our organization uses techniques to control bias during the interview process.

Strongly Disagree	Disagree	Neither Disagree or Agree	Agree	Strongly Agree

REFERENCE

Heneman, H.G., D.P. Schwab, J.A. Fossum, and L.D. Dyer 1989.
Personnel/Human Resource Management, 4th ed. Homewood, IL: Irwin, 351–352.

Generic Interview Evaluation Form

Please rate the candidate you have just interviewed. Complete this evaluation form immediately following the interview and send it to the CEO's office for review and tabulation.

Name of candidate:
Interviewed by:
Date interviewed:

Evaluation: Please give a numerical rating for each of the competencies or experiences below. Use the traditional 100-point scale, with 100 being the highest score possible and 0 being the lowest.

_____ Leadership skills
_____ Written communication skills
_____ Verbal communication skills
_____ Listening skills
_____ Executive presence
_____ Work ethic
_____ Related work experience
_____ People skills
_____ Ability to work with physicians
_____ Ability to relate to board members
_____ Ability to relate to community
_____ Technical skills and knowledge
_____ Project management skills
_____ Team relationship skills
_____ Creativity
_____ Negotiation skills
_____ Appearance

_____ Self-confidence
_____ Intelligence
_____ **Overall Rating**

Please describe in narrative form:

Strong points:

Weak points:

Interview Evaluation Form for Medical Director Position

The following criteria were developed to evaluate candidates for the medical director position. The criteria come directly from the position specification used to screen candidates. Following your interview with each candidate, please rate each candidate against each of the criterion.

Please complete this evaluation form as soon as possible after the interview and before comparing impressions with others. After the interview, please return this form to Jane Doe who is coordinating the interview process.

Please evaluate the candidate based upon a five-point scale, five (5) being the highest rating and one (1) being the lowest rating. If you are uncertain about an individual's qualifications for any criterion, please mark it "NE" for "not evaluated."

EDUCATION/CERTIFICATIONS

_____ Master's degree in business, health administration, or related area.

_____ Graduation from an AMA-accredited medical/osteopathic hospital.

_____ Educational course work in leadership and management (e.g., American College of Physician Executives courses or other programs).

PROFESSIONAL QUALIFICATIONS

_____ Minimum of five years clinical experience in a primary care setting.

_____ Maintenance of eligibility for medical staff membership at hospital including board certification in his/her primary specialty area.

_____ Maintenance of current license to practice medicine in the state and DEA certifications.

_____ Working knowledge of the primary care practice setting, including:

    _____ clinical aspects of practice

    _____ patient flow management

    _____ office/practice procedures

    _____ physician productivity

    _____ patient satisfaction and quality of care

_____ Knowledge of human development as it relates to interaction between caregivers and patients.

_____ Knowledge of current managed care practice issues (e.g., Milliman and Robertson standards).

_____ Ability to teach and guide others in application of standards.

_____ Written communication skills.

_____ Oral communication skills.

_____ Ability to work effectively as a team member.

_____ Prior experience interacting successfully with:

    _____ hospital management

    _____ physicians

    _____ outside organizations

_____ A professional and executive image.

_____ Demonstrates effective leadership traits by competently executing decisions.

_____ Ability to manage and run meetings.

_____ Computer literacy.

PERSONAL CHARACTERISTICS

_____ A high energy level.

_____ Understands the concept of mentoring and enjoys guiding and coaching others.

_____ A team player who regularly shares information.

_____ A secure, collaborative leadership style.

_____ Comfortable seeking counsel without losing decisiveness or the ability to take action and inspire others to take action.

_____ A facilitator who is sensitive to the ideas of others.

_____ Demonstrates the ability to lead a group, focusing them and energizing them to work together for change. This includes:

> _____ articulating an inspiring vision
>
> _____ the ability to manage resistance
>
> _____ the perseverance to carry through to completion

_____ Strives toward aggressive goals yet possesses a sense of reality.

_____ Focuses on current, objective realities, and on using an understanding of these realities to make decisions for the organization.

_____ Understands and gives appropriate emphasis to the long-term consequences of decisions.

_____ A strong record of follow-through.

_____ High ethical standards and the courage to act on his or her values and to take risks consistent with his or her values.

_____ **Overall Rating** (Not an average of the above scores but an overall impression)

Comments:

Candidate's name:

Interviewer:

Date:

CHAPTER 5

Making the Hiring Decision

"Deciding which of the candidates you've interviewed will make the best employee is never easy. The more successful you have been at attracting quality candidates, and at weeding out those who are clearly unqualified, the tougher the final choice is likely to be. The problem here is that the alternatives you have to choose among when you're making a hiring decision are not data you can feed into a computer."

—R. Half, 1985

WHEN MAKING THE final hiring decision, healthcare organizations face the following challenges:

- *Overcoming fear about making the decision.* Because of past hiring mistakes or the lack of a clear first choice, decision makers may "freeze" with fear and delay the hiring decision.
- *Aiming at or capturing a moving target.* Leadership teams often do not even look at the position specification when making the final hiring decision. This may be because not enough time was spent on its development or that it lacks enough specificity or detail to be helpful. Or, possibly, the decision makers do not consider it important. Worse yet, the position functions or qualifications, skills, or competencies may have changed, rendering the original specification obsolete. Interviews are often an educational process, and

as different candidates are introduced to the organization, opinions may change about what is needed for the position.

- *Controlling biases.* Chemistry, gut-feel, or appearance biases should not influence hiring decisions. This challenge is a huge one for most organizations. All too often, the final decision is based on an individual or group's gut-feel for the candidate.
- *Obtaining information critical to the hiring decision.* Because interviewers try to maintain a certain amount of decorum and respect during interviews, they may not ask the candidate the tough, difficult—but critical—questions.
- *Preventing "group think."* A false consensus can result if the choice of a final candidate is driven by the group.
- *Making a rational, good-fit decision.* At times, expediency can get in the way. The pressure to fill the position becomes so great that a quick decision is made. Worse yet, a candidate who is not fully qualified but better than the others in the pool is hired because the search team does not have the patience to start the search process all over again.
- *Making a timely decision.* The team must follow the established timetable for the interview and selection process. If delays in the process are allowed, such as when the decision-making time frame is delayed for several additional weeks, an organization can lose its best candidates. Matheny (1986) states this problem effectively:

There is a compelling reason why the search committee must reach agreement quickly at this point (after the final interviews). Up to now, presumably you have been carrying on dialogs with two or more individuals who are qualified, want the job, and would be successful if hired. You have to choose one with whom to proceed. But, if negotiations with that one are unsuccessful, you will want to proceed with the others. To preserve those options, you will have to move quickly or you will lose your candidates. What the process looks like to the candidates is this: they have been introduced to the company in a thorough and positive way by the information on the job and company provided them. They have responded properly to the information requests of the company. They have had several lengthy interviews with perhaps a number of people, who were well informed about them and the job and asked the right questions of them. Their interest has grown throughout the process to the point where they have provided references and other assurances. They now want to talk job offer. If you do not maintain their interest at this point, you will lose them. They will begin to build defenses against rejection. They will start thinking of why they should not take the job, rather than why they should. Changing companies, managers, products, problems, production facilities, cities, schools, homes, and friends—all of these considerations will turn into negatives.

ENHANCING THE SELECTION DECISION

Healthcare organizations most successful in gaining strong talent are those that take the final evaluation and selection stage seriously. They develop methodical ways to determine the best candidate. They create measures, where possible, craft interviews to ask for specific job-related questions, talk to references specifically about candidate accomplishments and attributes, and measure or evaluate the fit. A structured interview process and formal evaluation methods yield better information with which to make the final decision. A description of key strategies that can help to improve the decision-making process follows.

Identify critical elements of the selection decision

Boiling selection decisions down to their base elements is key to improving the decision-making process. Although many factors generally are involved in making any hiring decision, the following seem to be key:

- *Ability.* Ability may be judged based either on prior specific experience or the predicted ability to perform a job function.
- *Personality and fit.* These usually are determined subjectively by examining factors during the interview such as give and take, willingness to compromise, alertness, candidness, degree of poise, and the ability to be a good listener, to be assertive but not argumentative, pleasant, and relaxed.
- *Success factors.* Customized for each organization, these often entail an evaluation of people skills, leadership style, energy or work ethic, and achievement/goal orientation.
- *Urgency of filling the position.* This often plays a factor even though it may not seem to do so.
- *Dealing with negative concerns.* During interviews, small interpersonal flaws or imperfections may surface. Often a single specific incident or comment that is not clarified or explained in more detail "kills" consideration of a candidate. For example, one candidate for a human resources vice president position asked a group of executives who were interviewing her, Why should I come here? She was seeking their input about, and confirmation of, the many positive attributes of the organization; instead, they interpreted the question as an arrogant one.

As mentioned in chapter 2, a detailed position specification must be developed during the front-end preparation stage to avoid confusion about the critical elements of the selection decision.

Ask candidates for additional information and again, do not avoid the tough questions

No spoken or unspoken rule or law prohibits asking candidates for extra data or information following interviews. Interviewers might wish to ask candidates to provide copies of their annual reports to the board or reports to their supervisors. Although not done frequently, it is entirely reasonable to request copies of the candidate's performance evaluations. Many organizations conduct 360-degree evaluation processes, using the feedback for management and organizational development, performance appraisal, team development, and other purposes. If the candidate has been involved with this process, his or her feedback documents could be requested. For some candidates, it might also be appropriate to ask for actual work products. Marketing and public relations candidates often have portfolios of their work. Leaders can ask other candidates to provide the same (however, it is not inappropriate to ask for copies of an organization's audited financials). This type of additional information can aid those making the final assessment.

If there are doubts about a finalist candidate, again, follow-up conversation can be helpful to clear the air. Questions might include:

- Would you please describe further your role in your past two jobs? You have detailed specific accomplishments, yet we are unclear about your role with each. Would you please clarify? For example, were you the key leader or a team member for X, Y, or Z project?
- How would others describe your departure from your last position? You indicated that differences of opinion caused you to resign. Would others verify this or would some reference checks describe your departure as a termination?
- Would you kindly clarify for us the exact chronology of your job history, specifying months as well as years for each and every position you held?

Another technique used by some leadership teams is to fly the process leader to the town where the finalist candidate lives to ask him or her a final set of detailed and targeted questions. One CEO makes this a practice with all senior executive hires. She finalizes any concluding concerns she might have with a face-to-face discussion in the candidate's home location. If her concerns are addressed, she makes the final offer during the visit.

In essence, the task of those making the selection decision is to predict future job performance based on past performance. Obtaining answers to the following questions can be helpful in reviewing past experience.

- What was the candidate's exact role in the organization's achievements? How confident is the candidate in describing his or her role? Typically, candidates who actually functioned as a leader at the center of activities are quite detailed and confident in describing their roles. Those who were not are more ambiguous and uncertain with their descriptions.
- To what extent are the accomplishments truly measurable? Candidates who have played an active role in leadership positions can often cite specific numbers and facts related to goal achievement because they were integrally involved.
- What recognition, such as promotions, pay increases, incentive bonuses, and so forth, did the candidate receive in recognition of his or her accomplishments?
- To what extent does the candidate provide vague answers to certain questions? Examples include, I left for personal reasons, I was looking for additional responsibilities, or I had a values clash with my boss. These and other similar answers must be queried fully to address any concerns. Candidates need to understand that they likely will be eliminated from consideration if they do not address concerns in detail. In fact, it is critical during interviews to follow up these kinds of matters. For example, candidates could be told, "Quite frankly, for us to proceed further in this interview process, we need more details on your job history. Certain aspects of what you have given us do not seem to be as complete or understandable as we would like for us to advance your candidacy."

Conduct specific and customized reference checks

Reference checks can be very helpful because they give those making the selection decision an opportunity to talk with people who have spent days and hopefully months or years rather than hours with the final candidate(s). The goal of reference checking must be clear to the individual making the telephone calls, however. He or she may be trying to verify specific data to determine if the candidate has provided accurate information. For example, a reference might be contacted to inquire about the candidate's employment dates, compensation, reasons for leaving, or stated accomplishments. Or, the goal may be to get a sense for how the candidate performed in the past under stress or when faced with a challenging problem. The call also may focus on a specific issue or concern that surfaced during the interview process.

Individuals responding to potential employer's calls typically are not as forthcoming or direct as they once were. In fact, some people believe that reference checking is no longer valid because individuals are hesitant to say anything negative for fear of legal action by the candidate. Yet, crafted questions that deal with verification of facts and validation of experience can be gleaned from even the most hesitant references. For example, questions such as the following could be asked of references:

- Mary indicated that she directed the construction of the new heart hospital. It seems unusual for someone in her position to have done that. Would you please describe her role?
- Other references have suggested that under stress, John often loses the ability to re-prioritize and often gets behind in his commitments. Did this ever happen to him in your organization? Can you describe the situation?
- Would you please describe Susan's task force role? Was she simply a member of the team that redesigned the billing process or did she actually chair and lead that process?
- Did Bruce initiate the new performance appraisal process

and direct its implementation or, as CEO, did you come up with the idea and its implementation plan and he primarily responded?

- Quite frankly, we have already decided to hire Michael and we are just trying to determine areas where he might need additional coaching and support. Could you help us identify what these might be?

If the reference is critical to a vital selection decision, it is not unheard of for an employer or search consultant to travel to meet personally with the individual who could provide the key reference.

Conducting background checks for criminal history should also be considered. A recent example of why this can be important appeared in the press (Petersen 2001). The past conviction of the organization's top executive scientist caught one of the nation's largest medical device companies by surprise. His "distinguished" resumé was also distinguished by what it did *not* mention—a conviction for attempted murder and prison time at an Illinois correctional facility. Organizations can contact the Bureau of Criminal Investigations in their state. Some state bureaus can provide only information on criminal history in the state; others include checks based on the FBI's national database. A number of commercial companies conduct comprehensive background checks of criminal, credit, and other histories for a service fee.

Obtain and manage interview team input

As mentioned earlier, ensuring better selection decisions also requires obtaining and managing the input of the interviewing team. Many times, the senior team involved in the interview process will meet at the conclusion of all interviews to discuss the candidates. This approach has its strengths and weaknesses. On the positive side, it can enhance the spirit of teamwork and facilitate group decision making. On the negative side, it can stifle input from certain participants or result in "group think."

For example, if the CFO is a highly influential member of the executive team, other executives might wish to listen first to his or her comments before offering their own. If the CFO's comments about a candidate are positive, other executives might avoid mentioning negative points about the candidate. Or, team members might look for a signal from the CEO regarding who he or she prefers and then provide positive comments about only that candidate. One or more senior team members might dominate the conversation.

During evaluation meetings, the process leader must ensure that more verbal members do not sway less verbal ones. This can be achieved by structuring the group discussion process and by requesting thorough written evaluations prior to any group meetings. The leader can ask group members to provide their comments on one candidate at a time, round-robin style. Another approach is to appoint an advocate for each candidate so that one person in the room speaks on her or his behalf. Group discussion bias also can be minimized by presenting the results of the written evaluations and candidate ranking first, prior to starting the group discussion. At the end of the discussion period, some organizations conduct a secret ballot vote to obtain finalist candidate preferences from each team member.

The process leader should try to reconcile differing viewpoints. In some instances, votes should be weighed or weighted; in others, votes should be counted. This simply means that, while developing some consensus among senior team members or others involved in a selection decision, the person to whom the candidate will report needs to be able to veto a decision. That person's viewpoint should count and weigh the most. Selecting someone whom some people absolutely love while others absolutely hate can be problematic. However, settling for someone who is simply a safe choice may be a bad decision as well.

Determining in advance how the selection decision will be made can help to avoid the clash of different viewpoints. At times, a clash might be due to a single concern about the candidate. This could perhaps be resolved if the appropriate individual called the final candidate and said, "We are very comfortable with you in every respect except X. We need further clarification on this point and, if we obtain it, we can then move to an offer." If concerns linger and team members continue to be apprehensive about a candidate, it may be wise, in spite of time pressure, to start the search over.

Evaluate candidates using decision criteria and make a selection decision

The best selection decisions occur when leaders evaluate the candidates based on the decision criteria or critical elements of the selection decision identified earlier. The key challenge is to consider each element rather than to let one or two dominate the evaluation process. As described earlier, all too often, single specific comments or incidents that are not clarified or explained in more detail during an interview become the sole decision points. Poorly planned interviews that ramble without structure or without pursuit of information related to critical selection criteria exacerbate the human tendency to make a decision based on a single factor. All interviewers should try to minimize the weight that stray comments or behavior carry in final selection decisions.

The final evaluation process answers three key questions: What are we looking for? What are the skills, the competencies, the past experiences, and the personal fit and chemistry that will make a successful leader? How does this candidate rate with respect to all of these factors? Additional questions that can help guide the evaluation process include:

- Which candidate has worked in environments most like ours?
- Which candidate seems to mesh best with our leadership team? With whom was the team most comfortable?

- Which candidate has already completed in past jobs the key objectives that we need performed by the person in this job?
- Which candidate do we most trust?
- Which candidate has the clearest past record of relevant experience with no questions or concerns?
- Which candidate seems to be most excited about coming to join the organization? (Many experts advise never to hire someone who is running away from a job, but instead, to hire only those who are running toward the job that is being offered.)
- Which candidate would bring additional skills and strengths to the team and would complement the team as a whole?

Some organizations use a written evaluation tool to assist during the final evaluation process. An example appears as Appendix 5.1 at the end of this chapter. Note that this form combines factors from the position specification as well as more subjective decision points.

Evaluation of the candidate's values should be an important aspect of final selection. Very few organizations actually evaluate values as a part of a candidate's fit or chemistry. As one expert notes, "(In) the executive suite, where the accountabilities are less clear and often more abstract, leaders rely less on measurable qualities or results in selecting their successors. They may rely more on perceived potential, effort contributed to date, and the core values of the candidates" (Devries 1993).

Attention also must be focused on the timing of selection decisions. Moving too quickly or slowly can be harmful. The timetable established at the start needs to be followed.

If done properly, making the final selection decision will involve structure and science as well as subjective feelings. Ultimately, all selection decisions will contain an element of subjectivity. Selection is not a solely a science but an art *and* science. The better the preparation and the more planned the decision-making process, the better the decision and the union of art and science.

When it comes time to extend an offer, many organizations simply drop the ball. Fatigued from the high level of energy expended during the interview and evaluation stages, they handle the offer stage poorly. The most important aspects in making a final offer are speed, responsiveness, respect, sensitivity regarding the compensation and benefits package, and "downside protection." A description of each follows.

When the organization is ready to extend an offer, it must move quickly. Time delays between selecting the finalist candidate and extending an offer should be assiduously avoided. In addition, delays in getting back to candidates with answers to questions can often make the very best deals turn cold. Failure of either party to respond promptly to the other, like an engagement, can end the chance for a marriage. The offer should be extended verbally and followed up promptly in writing. Candidates cannot be expected to accept an offer made only verbally.

Communication with the individual selected should be highly responsive to the individual's questions and concerns. The finalist candidate and the executive making the offer should understand that the offer is not a take-it-or-leave-it proposition. Arrogance and organizational egotism expressed by the statement, "You should be glad we have selected you to work here," is a certain way to kill an offer. It shows a lack of basic respect.

The executive extending the offer must understand the sensitivity of the offer's financial aspects. Pay is very important to most people. At executive levels, the pay itself often becomes the measuring stick of the executive's success. Recent data indicate that candidates are less willing in a difficult industry like healthcare to move at all, and that significant pay jumps must be provided to get strong leaders to make a move. Data also show that many organizations are now "paying whatever it takes" to recruit new executives (Cotter 2001; American Hospital Publishing 2001). An increasing number of organizations are offering their key executives retention bonuses to keep them in place. The bottom line? The traditional 20 to 30% pay increase rule of thumb when an individual is changing organizations may now be outdated and ineffective. It is a seller's market; organizations must begin to act accordingly.

The individual extending the offer should provide full details on compensation, benefits, and incentive bonuses. One organization told a finalist candidate that he would have a "30% incentive plan," but failed to divulge that two-thirds of the amount had to be deferred and was not paid annually. Out-of-pocket costs of benefits should be described. Sometimes, organizations state, "We provide full relocation help," when in fact, they cover only moving truck expenses.

Use employment contracts

Executives who are offered the job may wish to receive an employment contract. Such a contract can protect them by providing a clear severance arrangement if the employment does not work out. A complete discussion of employment contracts is beyond this book's scope, but readers may wish to consult the ACHE publication *Contracts for Healthcare Executives* (ACHE 2002).

In brief, however, CEO and senior executive employment contracts are much more prevalent today than in the past. Sources suggest that the majority of CEOs have employment contracts. Those that *do not* usually have some type of employment letter that typically carries the same legal weight and significance as a contract (ACHE 2002). Employment contracts and comprehensive offer letters present the following benefits:

- They clarify expectations and conditions of employment, thereby reducing the likelihood of misunderstandings that can ruin employment relationships.
- They recognize that there is indeed a quid pro quo in an

employment relationship, even at the highest levels of the organization.

- They protect the prospective new executive, particularly at the CEO level, from changing opinions due to changes in board leadership.
- They protect high-level executives from the financial risks involved in moving geographically to take another job. Individuals who work at other levels in the organization can often find ample job opportunities without relocating their families.
- They can embolden executive decision making. The new executive does not have to fear immediate financial ruin for risky decisions. In this era of increased mergers and acquisitions and significant financial pressures, bolder decision making may be better for the organization.
- A clear employment contract can eliminate the contentiousness and hostile feelings that exist when an individual is terminated. Moreover, the costs of litigation can be minimized or eliminated entirely through the use of contracts.

Other industries have long provided employment contract protection. The healthcare industry should follow suit appropriately. Contracts and letters that set forth terms and conditions of employment typically cover the elements outlined in Appendix 5.2 at the end of this chapter.

Time lags involved in negotiating employment contracts or the details included in the offer-of-employment letter can create discomfort for both parties. If the organization or candidate is working with an outside attorney on the contract or letter, it may take longer than desired to iron out the details. Organizations should draft the contract or offer letter well in advance of making the final decision about who will be hired. If working with a search consultant, leaders should indicate the specific items that simply are not negotiable. Informing the candidates of these well in advance often avoids the impasses that can further delay or prevent finalization of the deal.

A word about severance might be helpful here. For reasons mentioned above, an employment contract with a severance arrangement protects the new leader. Some prospective hires could be reluctant to bring up severance, thinking that this kind of "prenuptial agreement" could suggest a lack of basic trust. However, they also should consider the financial and emotional costs of relocating family and home. It is not inappropriate to ask for protection. Some organizations are reluctant to provide severance. Such organizations might wish to consider placing severance within a time frame, such as offering one year of severance payments if the new leader is terminated during the first two years of employment.

Finally, it is important when dealing with contracts or the legal aspects of employment offers to seek the counsel of attorneys who are well versed in this area of law. Many local attorneys without access to national information simply do not have the expertise required to craft an appropriate employment contract or letter.

The offer stage is a very delicate one. Both sides often respond too personally to the specifics of an offer. The organization may be offended if the candidate does not accept the first offer. Or, the candidate may be offended if the organization does not respond quickly to a counteroffer. Most candidates at the executive level are already employed, and hence, may feel no need to accept the offer. If communication turns even slightly sour, the candidate may simply walk away. If the candidate's family is not excited about moving to a new city and leaving friends and other family, the issue can be compounded. Search consultants can serve as the intermediary, minimizing the personal feelings that often get in the way of a smooth negotiation. They can help move both sides to the final offer and acceptance. Chapter 8 addresses their role more fully.

CONCLUDING COMMENTS

Making the right hiring decision is one of the most important decisions that any executive will make. Simply put, when the decision is the right one, things go well; when it is not, the organization is often placed in turmoil. Organizations can minimize their risk of hiring mistakes by better understanding the factors that drive the hiring decision, asking tough and very directive questions during the interview process, and developing more objective approaches to the evaluation procedure.

EVALUATE YOUR ORGANIZATION

1. Our organization understands the key factors in making hiring decisions.

Strongly Disagree	Disagree	Neither Disagree or Agree	Agree	Strongly Agree

2. Our organization uses an objective process to make manager or executive hiring decisions.

Strongly Disagree	Disagree	Neither Disagree or Agree	Agree	Strongly Agree

3. Those interviewing candidates have no problem asking tough questions.

Strongly Disagree	Disagree	Neither Disagree or Agree	Agree	Strongly Agree

4. Our organization uses an effective strategy to evaluate the information we obtain during the interview process.

Strongly Disagree	Disagree	Neither Disagree or Agree	Agree	Strongly Agree

5. We effectively check the references of leadership candidates.

Strongly Disagree	Disagree	Neither Disagree or Agree	Agree	Strongly Agree

REFERENCES

American College of Healthcare Executives. 2002. *Contracts for Healthcare Executives,* 4th ed. Chicago: ACHE.

American Hospital Publishing. 2001. "Your CEO: Are You Short-Staffed or Short-Sighted?" *Trustee* 54 (7): 15–18.

Cotter, T. (of Sullivan Cotter and Associates). 2001. "The Healthcare Roundtable for CFO's." Presentation, Chicago, September 7.

DeVries, D.L. 1993. *Executive Selection: A Look at What We Know and What We Need to Know.* Greensboro, NC: Center for Creative Leadership, 25.

Half, R. 1985. *Robert Half on Hiring.* New York: Crown Publishers, 157.

Matheny, P.R. 1986. *Critical Path Hiring: How to Employ Top-Flight Managers.* Lexington, MA: Lexington Books, 43.

Petersen, M. 2001. "A Resume Distinguished by What It Didn't Mention. *The New York Times* September 6, A1, C6.

Chief Operating Officer
A Final Evaluation Guide

Candidate Name: _____

- Evaluate the candidate's specific past job experience, based on our key objectives, as follows:
  - Reengineer the medical staff organization.
  - Develop programs that will increase the retention rate of nursing and other professionals.
  - Evaluate outsourcing of dietary, housekeeping, and other support service departments.
  - Recruit new specialists.
  - Reengage the cardiologists and cardiothoracic surgeons in a renewed heart services marketing effort.
  - Working with finance, develop a more flexible budgeting system.

  Consider the candidate's past experiences and how he or she meets or doesn't meet our specific needs. Have the specific achievements described by the candidate been verified by references or other means?

- Evaluate the candidate's ability to assume additional responsibility.
  - Can he/she work independently?
  - Can he/she work with our board?
  - Has the candidate been able to assume added responsibilities in past jobs?
- Evaluate personal chemistry and fit.
  - Is the senior team unanimous on the candidate's selection? Is that unanimity strong? Weak?
  - Has anyone who interviewed the candidate identified any specific flaws or errors in judgment that might create

future problems? Have these been addressed through reference checks?
- Are the candidate's values compatible with organizational values?
- Evaluate objective factors.
  - Has the candidate's educational background been verified?
  - Have positions held and past dates been verified?
  - Are there other factors that require verification?
- Evaluate qualitative factors.
  - Have work ethic and typical hours of work been verified?
  - Does the health system psychologist indicate a fit within the culture and the leadership team?
  - Do family factors seem to be "in sync" with the needs of the position?
  - Have personal organizational ability and time management been evaluated?

Standard Items Covered in Employment Contracts or Letters

- *Term or length of the employment period.* This can run the continuum from no set term (employment at will) with or without a resignation/termination time period, for example, 30 or 60 or 90 days notice, to what is called an "evergreen" provision. This means that there is an end date on the term of the employment arrangement. Most CEO contracts carry a term of two or more years.
- *Severance.* This provision covers both the conditions under which the organization can terminate the executive, as well as the amount of continued salary and benefits that will be provided to that individual. Many contracts have some form of mitigation clause that states that following termination, some or all earnings from other employment sources will off-set payments from the terminating organization. This reduces the chance for "double-dipping," which is drawing a severance salary while also earning payment from a new employer. Mitigation clauses usually begin following at least twelve months of severance payment. The severance section also details the causes for termination. At times, these are loosely and poorly defined, such as "for just cause." This means that the cause for termination is an appropriate one if, in the eyes of the law, it is "just." Better severance language defines specific reasons for "just cause" termination, thereby minimizing the chance for lengthy litigation.
- *Duties.* This section identifies the functions, authority, and responsibilities of the position.
- *Compensation and benefits.* This details what the executive will be paid, what benefits are provided, and incentive compensation and other perquisites.

MAXIMIZING

LEADERSHIP

TALENT

CHAPTER 6

Learning the Ropes

"You've hired a new and highly qualified person to a key position in your company. You're happy; the new recruit is happy. That task is completed. Right? Well, not quite. You still have to bring the individual into the company and get this shining new executive off on the right foot with the rest of the people in the management organization. Aside from the usual routine of filling out forms, passing physician exams, and other necessary busy work, there is a procedure that should be followed whenever a new manager is hired."

—*P. R. Matheny, 1986*

EFFECTIVE TALENT MANAGEMENT requires recognition of the critical importance of how new leaders enter, acclimate and integrate within the organization. This process includes much more than orientation. It includes learning the norms and unwritten rules of behavior, dealing with initial "hazing," and adjusting to the stresses that typically come with new territory.

The process of "learning the ropes" can be critical to the success or failure of the new leader. Most healthcare organizations need to give much more thought than they currently do to the entry phase which often now can be characterized as haphazard and random. Once the selection decision is made and the offer extended and accepted, most organizations leave the new leader to his or her own devices to orient him or herself to learn about the organization and job. Some organizations have a limited management orientation program, but these usually are superficial and lack specificity, goals, or depth.

Some healthcare organizations approach the orientation of a new leader by simply suggesting that the new leader establish meetings with various other leaders and key individuals within and outside the organization. Through this approach, meetings are often left to chance, discussions during meetings may ramble because they lack clear objectives, and specific issues or problems may take precedence over the orientation discussion. Some meetings may be postponed or canceled and never get rescheduled. Although "around here-ism," informal information can be helpful to the new leader, time might be much better spent pursuing specific discussion objectives.

The new leader or manager frequently receives the organization's administrative policy manual and is asked to review it. Some healthcare organizations offer formal administrative orientation programs, often taught by staff who are not knowledgeable about high-level strategy and issues. Such orientations typically are not effective. In other organizations, the administrative assistant becomes the key person orienting the new manager or executive. Again, this approach to helping the new hire in his or her efforts to learn the ropes often leaves much ground uncovered.

IMPROVING THE ENTRY PROCESS

Healthcare organizations most successful in effectively integrating strong talent and getting those individuals up to speed quickly are those that take the entry stage of the leader's tenure with the organization seriously. They understand the challenges that the new leader faces, and make the entry and socialization process a formal one. A description of key strategies that can help to improve the leadership entry process follows.

Healthcare organizations should give serious thought to the issues that new leaders face when they first join organizations. Often "little things" create considerable challenge for new leaders. As Josefowitz and Gadon (1988) note,

> A lot more happens on the first day than appears on the surface. People sniff each other out, start testing one another; some will engage actively in conversation, others observe silently from a distance. How will each be to work with? Can that other be trusted? Will they collaborate or compete? Can you be up front or will you be taken advantage of? All these are unanswered questions: How do you find out? What do you look for? Whom do you ask? How do you become familiar with the unfamiliar? How do you get to be an old shoe and not feel your toes pinched every time you take a tentative step? How can you integrate better into the work place? How can you become effective faster—feeling "at home," part of the work group, a good team member?

Edgar H. Schein (1985), Emeritus Professor of Management at the Massachusetts Institute of Technology and considered one of the founders of organizational psychology, describes three stages of organizational entry: entry, socialization, and mutual acceptance. He also lists key challenges during the first two stages.

Stage 1 challenges for both the new leader and organization include:

- Obtaining accurate information in a climate of mutual selling.
- Avoiding the creation of false expectations. Even though both parties tend to focus on the long-term match, they may overlook the big picture by expecting quicker action in the early days or weeks.
- Learning that often there is a significant difference between what was portrayed in the interview process and what actually exists. This is one of the more dangerous aspects of entry because the new leader is often discouraged when this happens,

frequently feeling that he or she may have made a mistake joining the new organization.

Stage 2 challenges for the new leader include:

- Beginning to accept the reality of the human organization, including dealing with resistance to change, and how to work with others.
- Learning the organization structure and how it limits change, and often, dealing with too much or too little job definition.
- Learning to work with the new boss. Trust/mistrust and independence/dependence issues must be addressed.
- Understanding the real workings of the organization's reward system.
- Locating and establishing his or her place or identity in the organization.

While the leader is addressing these challenges, the organization is assessing how the individual fits and determining whether he or she will be an innovative contributor. The organization also is assessing how the new leader will learn and grow within the organization. A firm understanding of these issues helps organizations plan a more appropriate orientation for a new leader.

Design the process to meet the new leader's entry objectives

Healthcare organizations must understand and support the "psychology" of the leadership orientation process. During this process, the new leader is trying to establish an identity; selling his or her abilities, skills, and knowledge; evaluating the culture; assessing the need for change; and comparing the expectations that were communicated during the recruitment process with the organization's reality. The entry and socialization process should be designed to help the leader meet these objectives.

For example, one organization gives their new executives a time slot in the middle-management meeting agenda and other meeting agendas to present their objectives for their new role or job. This gives middle managers a chance to hear a formal presentation from new executives early in their tenure with the organization. It also enables the new executive to focus on the key early objectives that he or she will be addressing. Another CEO meets with her newly hired executives at the end of each month during the first five to six months. They specifically review the list of objectives that were set both during the interview process and during the first few weeks on the job. This allows interaction that is focused on the critical issues for the new executive's attention.

Make the process a formal one

As suggested throughout this book, formalizing processes can be *the* most effective improvement strategy. With entry and socialization, making the process a formal one involves building the process around the job's specific objectives. Goals for the orientation process, specific learning points, and timetables should be devised and implemented. The approach almost resembles a progressive, special college course curriculum, which takes the learner through a structured learning process with specified information content.

Provide information about the leadership team

Many leadership teams hold regular team-building management retreats and have taken various tests of leadership style, such as Myers Briggs (Myers et al. 1998) or Hogan (Hogan and Hogan

1995). With an enhanced knowledge of one another, these teams are able to improve their information sharing and group decision making. Providing the new leader with information from past retreats and exercises can be very helpful. For example, a large national bank holds twice yearly update sessions which include bringing new executives up to speed on team development activities. Resumés of team members are also useful to the new leader. A Midwestern manufacturing corporation actually keeps a binder with profiles of senior executives, their key objectives, and leadership styles. New executives review the binder when they begin with the company.

As an example in the healthcare arena, the vice president of organizational development at one Midwestern healthcare system spends focused time with new executives. He outlines in detail past leadership development activities that involved the senior leadership team and sets up lunches for the new executives that focus on conversing with different team members about past team-building activities.

Plan the new leader's introduction

The new leader needs to be introduced properly within the organization and to the community at-large. This involves doing more than an internal memo, an article in the organization's newsletter, or a press release for the community. Special thought should be given to welcome receptions and providing the new leader with an opportunity to make introductory comments at board and other management meetings. Thought should also be given to formal introductions at special events in the community and meetings of services clubs, the local chamber of commerce, and other community organizations. In order to facilitate community contacts, several healthcare organizations take new executives as guests to meetings of service clubs and other community organizations.

Be attentive to the new leader's family needs

Taking a new job, moving into a new community and house, and helping a spouse and children acclimate to a new job, school, and neighborhood, are at the top of most people's lists of factors that create stress. Often organizations forget about the family after the initial recruitment stage. Several healthcare organizations have formal plans to welcome new executives into the community by having selected spouses of current executives call the spouse of the new leader to invite him or her to lunch, coffee, or to parent meetings at the school. These organizations tend also to be very flexible in understanding the need for the new executive to have time off to help with the move and acclimate his or her family to the community.

Larger communities may have professional "welcome wagon" organizations with which the organization can contract to provide new leaders and their families ongoing support and help in getting oriented to a new community. Executives with children of similar ages and interests may wish to get together early in the new executive's tenure to ensure that questions are answered and guidance is given.

The key is not to leave such welcoming activities to chance, but instead, to make them formal, assign specific responsibility (often to the human resources executive or manager), and be certain that follow-up is completed. Being attentive to family needs may be as simple as

- making time during a meeting to address questions about the community,
- suggesting good family doctors, and then calling that physician to tell him or her that the new executive is going to be calling to schedule an appointment,
- taking the new executive and spouse on a tour of the community, or
- taking the new executive and spouse to golf or tennis at a local club and making introductions with club members.

Assign a mentor or buddy

Developing a "buddy" system with specific objectives and assigning a single individual the job of orienting a new senior manager or executive can be very helpful. This person need not take responsibility for the entire orientation program; others should be involved. An abridged version of one healthcare organization's buddy program appears as Appendix 6.1 at the end of this chapter. For a new CEO hire, the board chair might assume the mentor role. A search or strategy consultant, if used by the organization, or senior corporate counsel can play a valuable role in mentoring the new CEO.

Review progress in meeting critical objectives

Organizations should develop and implement a formal mechanism for reviewing progress with the new leader toward meeting the objectives outlined for the position. A review at the 30-, 90-, and 180-day points is appropriate. This gives both the new leader and his or her supervisor an opportunity to focus on specific objectives that may not yet have been addressed. Milestones dates should not pass without performance discussions between the new executive and his or her boss.

For example, the key first-year objectives for a new COO are to:

- Reengineer the medical staff organization.
- Develop programs that will increase the retention rate of nursing and other professionals.
- Evaluate outsourcing of dietary, housekeeping, and other support service departments.
- Recruit new specialists.
- Reengage the cardiologists and cardiothoracic surgeons in a renewed heart services marketing effort.
- Work with finance to develop a more flexible budgeting system.

Discussions between the COO and CEO at the 30-, 60-, and 90-day point should focus on progress toward meeting these specific goals. Performance review should directly correlate to discussions during the interview stage. More than simply an orientation process, the review focuses on the core issues that are critical to first-year success. One healthcare system worked with a consultant to identify behavioral expectations for the new CEO. The expectations were jointly developed by both the consultant and healthcare executives. These appear as Appendix 6.2 at the end of this chapter. The senior leadership team then evaluated the CEO based on these expectations.

CONCLUDING COMMENTS

With insight and humor, Matheny (1986) sums up the challenges of the entry process:

> The notion that a skilled and experienced executive will hit the deck running is naïve. The more experienced he or she is, the less likely that person is to hit the deck running. Even if the individual is from the same industry, practically everything is new—a new employer, new policies and procedures, new boss, new organization, new duties, new peers, new staff, new facilities, new products, new problems, and new company politics. If it is a new industry, throw in a couple dozen more "news." If it is in a new city, you can add a new home, new schools, new community, new acquaintances, and new problems and decisions to be made in day-to-day living for the spouse and children. Hit the deck running? Not on your life. Smart executives will creep around first and find out where the mine fields are laid, which is why you won't realize a whole lot of benefit from them in the first few months of employment. Anything you can do to speed up their learning process will pay big dividends.

EVALUATE YOUR ORGANIZATION

1. We have a formal management orientation process.

Strongly Disagree	Disagree	Neither Disagree or Agree	Agree	Strongly Agree

2. The formal management orientation process was developed with extensive senior management input, including the CEO's.

Strongly Disagree	Disagree	Neither Disagree or Agree	Agree	Strongly Agree

3. The management orientation process is appropriate for the new senior executive as well as the new middle manager.

Strongly Disagree	Disagree	Neither Disagree or Agree	Agree	Strongly Agree

4. Senior executives have the opportunity to learn about the backgrounds, leadership styles, and preferences of their senior management peers.

Strongly Disagree	Disagree	Neither Disagree or Agree	Agree	Strongly Agree

5. The family and social transition needs of new executives and managers are addressed during the orientation process.

| Strongly Disagree | Disagree | Neither Disagree or Agree | Agree | Strongly Agree |

6. Mentors or buddies are assigned to new leaders as part of the orientation process.

| Strongly Disagree | Disagree | Neither Disagree or Agree | Agree | Strongly Agree |

REFERENCES

Hogan, R., and J. Hogan. 1995. *The Hogan Personality Inventory*. Tulsa, OK: Hogan Assessment Systems.

Josefowitz, N., and H. Gadon. 1988. *Fitting In: How to Get a Good Start in Your New Job*. Reading, MA: Addison-Wesley Publishing Co., 12.

Matheny, P.R. 1986. *Critical Path Hiring: How to Employ Top-Flight Managers*. Lexington, MA: Lexington Books, 110.

Myers, I., M, McCaulley, N. Quenk, and A. Hammer. 1998. *Myers-Briggs Type Indicator Manual,* 3rd ed. Palo Alto, CA: Consulting Psychologists Press.

Schein, E.H. 1985. *Organizational Culture and Leadership*. San Francisco: Jossey-Bass. 91–92.

Buddy Orientation Guidelines

The primary purpose of our Buddy Orientation Program is to ensure that one person owns and manages the formal orientation of our new managers or executives. It is designed to ensure that new leaders are given an in-depth review of our practices, both formal and informal, and to help them acclimate socially.

General expectations include but are not limited to:

Prior to the arrival of the new manager/executive ("leader"):

- Meet with the new leader's supervisor to discuss key first-year objectives and identify initial issues/problems that the new leader will face. List any key orientation issues and determine the best method(s) to address each.
- Call the new leader to introduce yourself (if needed), to describe the Buddy Orientation Program, and to discuss thoughts, concerns, and issues. Ask the new leader if there are particular areas of interest that should be covered in an early orientation period. Discuss personal issues involved with moving, spouse relocation/job seeking, children's issues, schools, neighborhoods. Contact employment managers in human resources to ensure that any concerns that cannot be handled by the orientation buddy are addressed by human resources staff.

The following guidelines have been excerpted from the Buddy Orientation Guidelines used by a large Midwestern health system. The guidelines are part of a complete orientation/administrative manual that includes copies of all forms used by the organization. The orientation program is managed by human resources staff, but specific vice presidents and other selected senior managers are assigned as orientation managers or buddies. The human resources vice president conducts a brief training program with any vice president or manager assigned to be a buddy. Buddies are assigned based on expected compatibility.

Day One:

- Meet the new leader for breakfast or coffee and then escort him or her to his or her supervisor's office for their initial meeting.
- Arrange for a group lunch with two or three other managers/executives.
- Meet with new leader and vice president of human resources to discuss team members' history, backgrounds, leadership styles, and organizational traditions.

Day Two:

- Establish formal learning objectives for the orientation program and address any questions.

Weeks One to Three:

- Weeks one and two. Ensure that the new leader has lunch partners if desired.
- Week one. Review the list of all meetings the new leader will attend, their purpose, their regular attendees, and discuss the role of the leader with these groups.
- Weeks two and three. Arrange orientation meetings with purchasing agent, human resources generalist, accounts payable manager, and payroll manager to cover organizational policies, forms and processes.
- Week three. Review initial objectives of orientation program, meeting schedules, and evaluate progress.

First Month:

- Ensure attendance at the health system orientation program. Attend the orientation lunch to sit with the new leader.
- Arrange a dinner at a local restaurant to include spouse and another couple.

- End of month one. Meet with new leader's supervisor to determine orientation progress. Hold follow-up meeting with new leader.

Expectations for a CEO

The following lists are reasonable behavioral expectations that a senior management leadership team might have of their CEO. Obviously, these kinds of behaviors are rarely discussed between CEO and senior executives; usually, the presence of an outside coach or mentor is necessary to elicit this type of feedback.

As part of the search process for the CEO at Alpha Health System, an agreement was reached with the board chair, the new CEO, and search consultant to engage in an ongoing mentoring/coaching/team-building process to enhance the performance and effectiveness of the senior leadership. Additionally, it was agreed that the search consultant would assist in the design of the CEO evaluation process to be used by the board.

The most appropriate type of evaluation is one that focuses on what is expected beforehand; in other words, an evaluation is performed after a period of time passes during which the individual being evaluated is aware of the expectations for that time period. In essence, the design of the process should ensure no surprises.

BEHAVIORAL EXPECTATIONS OF THE CEO

The following behavioral expectations are designed to elicit consideration of the CEO's effectiveness with the senior team. Prior to the evaluation of the CEO by the board, each senior team member will be asked to score the CEO on the following behavioral expectations. This evaluation will be completed and returned to the search consultant and aggregated for a cumulative assessment. This will provide part of the data input for the board evaluation of the CEO.

The CEO Builds Relationships

- The CEO stays in touch with people at all levels.
- The CEO stays in touch with the senior leadership team.
- The CEO gives timely and appropriate feedback.
- The CEO is approachable.
- The CEO respects individual differences in perspective and background.
- The CEO listens and considers perspectives from a broad range of individuals.
- The CEO recognizes and appreciates the needs and concerns of other people.
- The CEO takes personal steps to preserve and maintain personal relationships, even when there is conflict and heated situations.

The CEO Encourages Trust

- The CEO practices what he or she preaches.
- The CEO maintains high personal integrity.
- The CEO maintains personal standards under stress.
- The CEO establishes fair and consistent practices.
- The CEO is collaborative.
- The CEO demonstrates trust in others by delegating and listening to their viewpoints.
- The CEO is not self-absorbed.
- The CEO demonstrates candor.
- The CEO admits mistakes and limitations.
- The CEO practices forgiveness and reconciliation.
- The CEO does not give in when it compromises integrity.

The CEO Empowers Others

- The CEO creates "stretch" expectations, but ones that are reachable.
- The CEO reinforces risk-taking by not "killing" mistake-makers.
- The CEO creates a feeling of energy, excitement, and personal investment.
- The CEO ensures that the environment has a sense of purpose and direction.
- The CEO creates an environment of accountability.
- The CEO gives senior managers the chance to run their operations.
- The CEO backs the leadership team.
- The CEO promotes collaboration.
- The CEO takes the time to celebrate.
- The CEO recognizes the contributions of the team.

The CEO Possesses and Practices a Contemporary Contingency Leadership Style

- The CEO is not rigid and exhibits an adaptable leadership style.
- The CEO assesses each situation and each person in a situation and reacts accordingly and appropriately.
- The CEO exhibits a variety of leadership styles when appropriate (supportive and encouraging; driving and demanding; hands-off and delegating; or participative).

The CEO Is Emotionally Intelligent

- The CEO reads and understands his or her emotions and how they affect work performance and relationships.

- The CEO has a degree of humility.
- The CEO sets realistic standards for him- or herself.
- The CEO presents a positive outlook.
- The CEO anticipates stress and reacts appropriately.
- The CEO takes objective and systematic approaches to issues.
- The CEO stays open to feedback.
- The CEO explains unpopular decisions to others.
- The CEO maintains a sense of humor.
- The CEO readily shares credit and gives others opportunities for visibility.
- The CEO solicits feedback.
- The CEO acknowledges his or her mistakes and limitations.
- The CEO controls his or her emotions and keeps impulses under control.
- The CEO is skillful at sensing the emotions of others, understands their perspectives, and respects their concerns.

The CEO is Adaptable and Adept in Manifesting Different Approaches to Different Situations

- The CEO works constructively and calmly under stress and pressure.
- The CEO focuses on priorities.
- The CEO works effectively in ambiguous situations.
- The CEO takes calculated risks.
- The CEO copes effectively with politics.
- The CEO transforms competition into collaboration, when appropriate.
- The CEO creates a positive political climate.
- The CEO handles tense situations without overreacting or becoming overly emotional.
- The CEO practices appropriate conflict management skills.

The CEO Communicates

- The CEO practices a balanced blend of talking and listening.
- The CEO shares information appropriately.
- The CEO speaks with precision and clarity and clarifies ambiguous messages.
- The CEO encourages open and frank discussions of issues.
- The CEO is able to express opinions without intimidating others.
- The CEO is open to opposing viewpoints.

The CEO Attracts and Develops Leadership Talent

- The CEO recruits strong leadership talent.
- The CEO builds a balanced team.
- The CEO sets clear expectations.
- The CEO provides direct, clear, and timely constructive feedback.
- The CEO provides positive feedback and recognition.
- The CEO supports development.
- The CEO confronts problem performers directly and replaces them when appropriate.

The CEO Is an Appropriate and Timely Decision Maker

- The CEO is not hesitant to make decisions.
- The CEO balances decision making and analysis.
- The CEO is an integrative decision maker.
- The CEO assigns clear accountability in decision-making processes.

CHAPTER 7

Leadership Development

"The development or continued preparation of our managers and executives is by far the most important thing we can do for the future of our organization—but we fund it poorly, we fail to plan for it, and when we do provide programming, we all act as though it is the last item on our action agenda. As the environment becomes more challenging, I worry that we will pay a high price for this."

—CEO of a large health system

A HEALTHCARE ORGANIZATION has identified prospective leadership talent to fill its vice president or director of clinical services or another position. The recruitment process proceeds smoothly and a number of quality internal and external candidates express interest in the job. Candidates are evaluated based on solid criteria and a top candidate is identified. The offer extended to this individual is accepted and the senior leadership team effectively orients the new executive to his or her responsibilities and the organization. Now what? Effective talent management requires continuing leadership development.

The best solution to the healthcare leadership shortage may be the "grow your own" solution. A program designed to identify potential "move-up" leaders, assess their competencies and shortcomings, and offer developmental and experiential learning opportunities may be one of the best strategic initiatives an organization could focus on in the next decade.

Traditionally, healthcare organizations have not moved many people up into senior positions. However, almost all first-line supervisors in healthcare organizations are hired from the inside. Experts suggest that approximately two-thirds of middle-management positions are filled with internal candidates, and almost no senior-level positions are filled from the inside. Reasons for these trends include:

- There is less risk of making a hiring mistake at the first-line supervisory and middle management levels because opportunities to observe candidates abound, resulting in more objective assessment of skills;
- The work of first-line supervisors and middle managers is more similar to the work of their direct reports than is the case with senior executives; and
- It is logistically difficult to allow middle managers to "try out" the duties of an executive position for a short period of time.

Healthcare organizations have done a poor job of management and leadership development. Typical approaches include management training classes that are often taught by inexperienced staff education associates. Rarely is the content very sophisticated and the more senior the manager, the less attractive the courses. Other approaches include offering financial support for attendance at programs sponsored by various health and managerial societies and associations. Some organizations offer to pay a portion of the costs of MBA or other masters degree programs, viewing this as their management development program.

Unlike other industries where promising leadership talent has ample opportunity to work in several areas of the company, healthcare organizations typically do not offer job rotations across job functions. The primary reason is that each of the executive areas, and managerial areas as well, are much more tied to specialty areas of knowledge. In fact, many leadership positions require licensure or certification. For example, a nursing license may be required for the chief nursing officer and a CPA for the CFO.

The relative size of the organization is also a factor. Organizations in industries that offer job rotations typically are large, often having well in excess of 40,000 employees. Even the largest healthcare organizations are much smaller than this. Until the mergers of the 1990s, it was rare to find any healthcare organization larger than 4,000 or 5,000 employees. Even today, the largest healthcare organizations have approximately 20,000 employees. Job rotations are easier to offer in large organizations due to the increased depth of upper management ranks. For example, at Procter & Gamble, there likely are 10 to 15 highly capable people reporting to the corporate CFO who have complete knowledge of all the company's finances. In contrast, at a large healthcare organization, no one beyond the CFO typically has a comprehensive picture of the organization's finances. Job rotation in smaller organizations simply is more difficult to implement. However, this should not preclude its use, as described later in the chapter.

Mentorship of young managers "on their way up the ladder" has been declining in healthcare. Many senior executives state that, given the current healthcare environment, they simply do not have the time to spend with younger managers. In today's turbulent healthcare world, senior executive suites often resemble disaster command centers where immediate concerns are being addressed. Because of the potential mentors' need to focus on managing the short and long-term survival of their organizations, many new graduates and future leaders do not have role models or the chance to interact with senior-level executives.

Finally, promotional pay increases tend to be more generous when a person moves to another organization and less generous when moving up from within. Often, organizations behave rather bureaucratically when considering pay increases for individuals who are promoted from within. They frequently will pay an internal candidate far less than what they would pay if they recruited someone from the outside. This often discourages executives and managers from seeking upward movement within their own organizations and undercuts management development programs.

ENHANCE AND IMPROVE LEADERSHIP DEVELOPMENT

Healthcare organizations most successful in retaining strong talent are those that take the leadership development process seriously. They identify highly effective middle managers who should be groomed for senior-level positions and develop a formal leadership development program for these individuals and involve senior leaders in the program. They study the leadership development programs offered in other industries. They commit to promoting from within and they provide the resources necessary to ensure a successful leadership development program. A description of each of these key strategies follows.

Develop and implement a process for identifying future leaders

Many companies outside of healthcare build successful leadership development or succession planning programs by identifying strong leadership talent currently working at lower levels in the organization. This requires a formal process. Highly effective middle managers are identified and targeted for attention and growth by senior leadership. Many companies that do a good job with leadership development use a senior management committee that is empowered to review lists of managers capable of upward progression or preparation for upward progression on an annual basis. A human resources staff member normally tracks the progress of the up-and-comers, noting formal educational development, progress with mentors or coaches, and exposure provided to broader areas of the company's operations. Early in the identification process, most companies inform these individuals that they have been recognized as persons with strong potential for future growth within the company.

In healthcare, the approach typically is a less formal one. Senior executives, often the CEO or the COO, identify middle managers—usually clinical ones, such as directors of pharmacy, radiology, or laboratory services—who seem to work well with projects, run efficient departments, and perhaps have strong relationships with physicians. They expand the duties of these individuals.

What criteria are and should be used to identify future leaders? The performance of the units for which the managers are responsible should be the first and foremost criterion. If areas are operating successfully according to the success measures used by the organization, the individual managing the area should be noticed. Senior leaders initially may give such managers special projects to handle and then assess their performance with these. Following this, the leadership potential of up-and-coming managers can be assessed formally, their aptitude and leadership style measured, and their knowledge deficiencies determined so that they might receive additional education. A sample set of criteria appear as Appendix 7.1 at the end of this chapter.

Create a program that addresses senior management learning needs as well as those of middle management

Successful leadership development programs provide both senior and middle-level managers with customized developmental and experiential learning. The programs groom all participants for promotional opportunities. Healthcare organizations often neglect to target the senior leadership group for leadership development, or they allow each senior manager to carve out his or her own personal program of growth. The result? Often, nothing occurs. Senior managers need to receive continuing education and all of this education should not come from beyond the organization. An experienced advisor, counselor, or consultant who is qualified to teach leadership and highly respected by the senior team can teach the formal courses. Some well-known healthcare organizations spend significant money bringing in national speakers and experts to provide in-depth interaction with the senior group. Examples of leadership development curriculums appear as Appendices 7.2 and 7.3 at the end of this chapter.

Some organizations develop ongoing relationships with psychologists or consultants who work closely with senior team members on team functioning and other topics. The consultants meet frequently with senior team members, both individually and in groups, and serve as an "outside mirror" in coaching, guiding, and providing feedback on how the leaders are functioning. They identify areas of conflict that need to be addressed, and then manage the group through the conflict resolution process. Psychologists often use leadership tests that provide some basis for initial interaction. A professional from outside the organization—someone who does not have the same risks of opening up that team members do—often can effectively help the leadership group achieve significant growth and development.

Involve senior leaders

Successful leadership development requires the participation of senior executives. These individuals must be visibly and actively involved. Some senior executives may be qualified to teach portions of the program and they certainly should be at the table when material relevant to their own leadership growth is presented. For example, the CFO could teach financial management in the hospital's or health system's internal management education program. Other executives could participate as well. This gives them an opportunity both to share their areas of expertise and to interact with middle-level managers, thereby removing some of the mystique that often accompanies high-level leaders.

Leaders of healthcare organizations can learn a great deal by exploring how other industries approach leadership development. They should give serious consideration to the management rotation programs used at Procter & Gamble, IBM, GE, Hewlett Packard, and other companies. It is not unusual for senior executives in these companies to spend 18 to 24 months working in each area of the company, including finance, sales, business development, human resources, or line operations. The companies indicate that this kind of in-depth exposure creates leaders who are better rounded and have a deeper understanding of all aspects of company management. The exposure also may curb biases that occur when an individual has knowledge of only a single area of the company. Vertical career movement—up the ladder in only one area of the company—can inhibit leadership development. "One of the things that the best organizations do consistently is (provide) a lot of horizontal movement," write two management experts (Bennis and Townsend 1995).

Who said the pharmacy director cannot manage radiology? Although rotation may not be as easy at the executive level in healthcare, movement among operations positions can help the organization avoid segmenting duties into such "boxes" as professional services, clinical services, and support services. For example, when the vice president of nursing at one healthcare organization left for a two-month medical leave, senior leaders decided not to take the usual approach of appointing one of her directors, who were all relatively new to their roles, to serve in an interim capacity. Instead, the vice president of human resources moved into the nursing vice president's office and the director of human resources moved up to be the vice president of human resources on an interim basis. The vice president of human resources successfully managed nursing for the two-month period. In another organization, the director of pharmacy assumed the chief information officer role for nine months while a new CIO was being recruited. With a firm understanding of information technology issues, the pharmacy director was able to do the job successfully. Rotations need not take place only in instances of vacancies or medical leaves, but should be considered on an ongoing basis.

Commit to promoting from within, whenever possible

If potential leaders are effectively identified within the organization, and if the developmental programs succeed in advancing the knowledge, skills, and experience of talented individuals, promotions from within must take place. The senior leadership team must commit to promoting from within, whenever possible. Interim appointments may be appropriate in order to give individuals a trial period with little risk. After leaders successfully promote from within once or twice, the development and promotion of internal candidates will become an integral part of the organization's succession planning program described later in this chapter.

Create opportunities for managers to expand the scope of their responsibility

Leadership development requires giving promising managers and executives the opportunity to perform tasks outside their normal areas of authority. At the senior level, executives often are given opportunities to run areas outside their usual areas of responsibility. For example, one hospital gave its chief human resources officer the responsibility of operating its management services corporation. At the middle-manager level, interdisciplinary task forces can give promising individuals the chance to work on projects beyond their normal day-to-day areas of responsibility. For example, organizations that are beginning a major building program, such as a new Women's and Infant's Center, could appoint a middle manager to chair the process. Some healthcare organizations establish a human resources committee comprised of middle managers to give counsel to the chief human resource officer on matters of personnel policy, compensation, and employee relations. Chairing these committees can provide excellent opportunities to demonstrate leadership.

Leaders should consider ways to expand the authority given to middle managers. All too often in healthcare organizations, there is *too much* authority high in the organizational structure and *not enough* authority lower in the structure.

Provide the resources necessary for leadership development

Healthcare organizations should maintain a strong education and travel budget. In addition to leadership time, financial resources are critical to successful leadership development. Healthcare organizations typically maintain a minuscule budget for such purposes. According to a number of CFOs, healthcare education and travel budgets rarely exceed 2 to 3 percent of the total organizational budget. In other industries, the number often reaches 8 to 9 percent of total expenses.

Typically in tough times and often for symbolic reasons, travel and education budgets are the first to be cut. "In difficult times, our executives need to be here minding the store and not out traveling to some resort location," remarked one CEO. Although it is appropriate to be sensitive to the location of programs, an opposite viewpoint should be taken. In tough times, leaders need to be out and about, networking, eliciting new ideas, growing and developing, and rejuvenating themselves through professional contact.

Develop leadership measures

Effective healthcare organizations measure what they do in order to improve their performance and ensure the effectiveness of improvements. Like all organizational processes, leadership and leadership development should be measured and improved. Leadership measures might include, among others, employee satisfaction, patient satisfaction, employee turnover, employee retention or average length of service, and timely completion of budgets and projects.

Unfortunately, many people view leadership development as "just a lot of talk." Most leaders go about their day-to-day activities without fully understanding what they are doing or where they are heading. Dick DeVos (1997), president of Amway, wrote that, "Leadership is one of those roles people sometimes accept without understanding the responsibilities they carry." DeVos is passionate about measurement—about knowing exactly where he is going and how to know when he has arrived. He also obviously believes that too many leaders do not fully comprehend the serious nature of leadership responsibility.

SUCCESSION PLANNING

Leadership development is closely related to succession planning. In essence, *succession planning* is a formal process that:

- Identifies key leadership positions that should remain filled at all times, if at all possible;
- Identifies individuals in such positions who, for whatever reason, are likely to leave soon;
- Identifies potential internal candidates to fill those positions and their development and experience needs; and
- Provides educational and experiential opportunities to address these needs.

A study by the Governance Institute (1997) indicated that only 10 percent of healthcare organizations have formal board-approved CEO succession plans. Probably fewer have succession plans that address positions below the CEO level. Some healthcare organizations may not have formal succession planning programs but their boards or senior teams do discuss leadership succession. Often organizations do not have formal succession plans because of the extreme sensitivity of the planning process and the difficulty of keeping it confidential.

Leadership development is critical to succession plans. Prospective senior leaders must be provided with educational programs, in-depth exposure to other areas of the organization, and expanded authority.

CONCLUDING COMMENTS

Practically all would agree that the most effective organizations in healthcare or any other industry are those that place a high emphasis on leadership development. The growth, development, and advancement of the leaders of any organization should be one of the top strategic priorities. Built on this foundation should be a formalized program of management and leadership succession.

EVALUATE YOUR ORGANIZATION

1. On at least an annual basis, our board reviews the educational and developmental programs for leadership development.

Strongly Disagree	Disagree	Neither Disagree or Agree	Agree	Strongly Agree

2. The growth and development of managers and executives is an ongoing topic at the senior management level.

| Strongly Disagree | Disagree | Neither Disagree or Agree | Agree | Strongly Agree |

3. The organization provides the financial resources necessary for leadership development.

| Strongly Disagree | Disagree | Neither Disagree or Agree | Agree | Strongly Agree |

4. The organization values and encourages continuous learning.

| Strongly Disagree | Disagree | Neither Disagree or Agree | Agree | Strongly Agree |

5. Individuals at levels higher than first-line supervisor have been promoted from within.

| Strongly Disagree | Disagree | Neither Disagree or Agree | Agree | Strongly Agree |

6. The organization defines leadership attributes and measures leadership and leadership development results.

| Strongly Disagree | Disagree | Neither Disagree or Agree | Agree | Strongly Agree |

7. The board and senior leaders discuss succession planning.

Strongly Disagree	Disagree	Neither Disagree or Agree	Agree	Strongly Agree

REFERENCES

Bennis, W., and R. Townsend. 1995. *Reinventing Leadership: Strategies to Empower The Organization*. New York: William Morrow and Co., 145.

DeVos, D. 1997. *Rediscovering American Values*. New York: Dutton, 248.

The Governance Institute. 1997. "CEO Succession Planning." La Jolla, CA: The Governance Institute, Fall.

Alpha Health System
Middle Management Progression
Criteria

Alpha Health System has established a progression program to identify highly successful leaders from our middle-management ranks. Once each year, one or two middle managers will be identified for this program. Once selected, these individuals will be given additional exposure to other operating areas of Alpha Health System, will receive extra educational program opportunities, may be provided additional chances to attend outside seminars, and will be assigned a coach from the senior management ranks for guidance. Selected middle managers will be given opportunities to attend meetings of the senior leadership team, the medical executive committee, and board meetings.

The criteria used to determine acceptance in the program are:

- Nomination by and complete support of immediate supervisor.
- Measured success over time in areas of authority, including success with implementing budgets, enhancing staff morale, reducing staff turnover, and achieving results through cooperation with other departments.
- Evidence of active participation and leadership in middle-management projects.
- Evidence of active participation and leadership in community activities such as United Way or membership on a voluntary board, such as the American Heart Association, American Cancer Society, and so forth.
- Emotional intelligence, as determined by comments of support from peers and those supervised.

- Completion of formal and informal leadership development programs, such as advanced degrees and seminars.
- Participation and leadership in the development of leadership development programs within the organization.
- Evidence of a flexible and adaptable leadership style.
- Preparation of staff within the department who can assume the middle manager's responsibilities.

Sample Core Curriculum for Leadership Development

Leaders at Alpha Health System must successfully complete each of the courses in the core curriculum to earn the program certification. The courses are as follows:

Management Orientation

This orientation prepares new supervisors and managers to effectively manage people at work by providing fundamental information required by the supervisor or manager to make people both more productive and more satisfied with their working life.

Managing for Commitment

This program teaches supervisors and managers how to use positive reinforcement to enhance employee performance. Sessions are designed to build practical management skills in performance coaching and developmental feedback.

Essential Service Management

This course teaches supervisors and managers how to instruct, guide, and prompt employees to provide excellent customer service.

Communicate to Motivate

This course teaches supervisors and managers how to positively influence others through effective communication.

Delegating

This course teaches supervisors and managers how to recognize the need to delegate, provide guidance appropriate to employee's competence and experience, and establish supportive controls.

First Things First

This course teaches supervisors and managers how to manage multiple priorities in their work as well as their lives.

High-Impact Performance Appraisal

This course gives supervisors and managers the attitudes, knowledge, and skills that impact the effectiveness of performance appraisals.

Behavioral Interviewing

This course teaches supervisors and managers how to prepare, conduct, and follow-up a behavioral interview.

Tools and Techniques for Solving Quality Problems

This workshop expands thinking and directs creativity toward identified goals and objectives, realistic data collection, and enables individuals to select the most practical and cost-effective solutions.

Gateway to Leadership

This course identifies the skills and attitudes necessary for a supervisor or manager to start the transition from being a manager to being a true leader in the organization.

Sample Leadership Development Courses

Management Excellence

This course presents management and leadership expectations as driven by the organization's mission, values, culture, and initiatives. Participants develop a business plan to assure alignment of their departments' services, goals, and priorities with the strategic direction of their health system business unit.

Managing Quality

This course covers the manager's role in continuous performance improvement. Participants develop indicators that measure their departments' key dimensions of customer satisfaction, quality, operational performance, and financial outcomes.

Discipline Without Punishment

This course introduces managers to the principles and applications of the discipline process. Participants learn techniques to use in developing acceptable employee performance, including a five-step coaching process.

Performance Management Through Planning and Communication

This course introduces managers to the philosophy and principles of pay for performance and the guiding framework for the Health System's performance planning and appraisal system. Participants learn how to develop individual performance plans that are aligned with the aspects of the job, the department goals, and personal development needs.

Success Factors: Interviewing for the Right Fit

This course gives managers the tools for hiring the best candidates for a job by identifying success factors which help to determine a candidate's technical, cultural, and motivational fit for a job.

Team Building for Managers

This course addresses the manager's role of leading a work unit. It covers areas such as gauging the chemistry of the group, understanding group dynamics, and assessing team strengths and weaknesses. It focuses on the critical skills required for team development.

SEARCH

METHODOLOGIES

CHAPTER 8

Search Committees

"Search committees can often be the key to selecting a values- oriented leader."

—*S. F. Fritsch, 1992*

"Search committees can do a wonderful job or they can do a terrible job. The difference often comes down to how carefully they are set up and how closely they are managed. Unfortunately, most organizations just wind them up and let them go."

—*CEO of a large midwestern health system*

THE HEALTHCARE INDUSTRY, similar to higher education, is well known for its use of search committees. Practically every CEO search involves a search committee comprised of board members. Search committees are used increasingly with many medical staff and physician executive searches, and executive searches overall. Why are search committees used? The underlying rationale usually entails the desire to provide multiple constituents with a voice in the decision-making process. When the position to be filled involves serving the needs of a larger population than that of a single-line manager or supervisor, many organizations use the search committee approach.

Although the use of search committees can be very effective in recruiting, the process itself becomes more complex and requires careful monitoring. Search committees usually suffer from the following problems:

- Delays and confusion often abound because no one person manages the process. The protracted search timeframe can harm the organization, create problems for individuals serving in interim roles, and allow good candidates to slip through the cracks because their candidacy is not acted on quickly enough.
- Often appointed for political or symbolic reasons, the chair of the search committee has little authority and, due to other substantive duties, may not have the time to devote to a complex search.
- The best candidate may not be picked because the committee wants to reach a consensus decision. Instead, the candidate who seems to offend the least people is selected. Compromise candidates are often mediocre.
- The deliberation process frequently is superficial because committee members may not be comfortable saying what they actually think about candidates.
- In many cases, search committees are not truly empowered with authority for the selection process. The final selection takes place behind the scenes, creating feelings of intrigue and political maneuvering.

Perhaps the term *selection committees* or *screening committees* would more accurately describe the real work typically performed by search committees.

ENHANCING THE PERFORMANCE OF SEARCH COMMITTEES

Healthcare organizations can effectively use search committees to fill key leadership positions. However, the leadership and composition of the committee itself must be of high quality and a clear search process and definitive timetable must be established and followed. A description of strategies vital to the successful functioning of search committees follows.

Determine why a search committee is being used

As simple as this might sound, spelling out in advance why a search committee is being used can greatly enhance the committee's success. Questions such as these should be asked and answered:

- Has the search committee been assembled primarily to give a wider audience a voice in determining selection criteria? Is the committee expected to help "open up" the hiring process by removing potential mystery or secrecy? Or, is the committee's purpose to help identify potential candidates?
- What is the search committee's authority? Has it been granted an advisory or a decision-making capacity? Do all committee members understand and accept the committee's authority?
- Do the organization's leaders expect the search committee to improve the quality of the selection decision? If so, how?

Appoint a process manager

A process manager functions as a facilitator for the search process and, most often, should be someone other than the committee's chair. The process manager must be objective and skilled at moving the committee along toward its goal. He or she should encourage open communication and broad participation and should have the power and authority to push the committee forward in its work and to address sensitive issues that may arise.

The process manager needs to be a seasoned individual with relatively high-ranking status within the organization. It is very beneficial if the individual has recruitment and selection expertise. The person may come from the organization's human resources division. It is best if the process manager is not a "stakeholder" in the decision-making process. Ideally, this person should not have voting privileges because of potential conflicts of interest and the possibility of holding more sway over the process than appropriate. The process manager should attend all committee meetings. He or she should be tied in some way to the authority who appointed the committee. The committee must know that the process manager is speaking on behalf of the authority that appointed him or her. For example, if a process manager is facilitating a search process on behalf of the CEO, the search committee needs to know that he or she speaks for the CEO, that he or she is regularly apprising the CEO of the search committee discussions, and that he or she carries needed messages back and forth between the committee and the CEO. In essence, the process manager is serving as the CEO's agent.

All too often, a management intern or fellow is given process management duties and asked to be the "aide" to the search committee chair. An individual at this level does not have the tenure or organizational clout to handle many of the issues that arise during a search process, such as discussions of salary, executive benefits, or sensitive matters of reporting relationship or authority.

Appoint the right chair

The right person to chair a search committee is one who has authority and is effective in drawing out thoughts and input from all committee members. A dictatorial or forceful person is *not* the right choice. Such a person might be able to get the process moving, but could undermine the efforts of committee members and create divisiveness during the final selection steps. A person who, wanting everyone to be happy, is unable to build or achieve group consensus is also *not* the right choice because the committee could become frozen and unable to make a decision in a timely fashion.

Appoint the right committee members

Search committee members must be appointed for the right reasons. Naming members for political or symbolic reasons creates problems. So does appointing members based only on representational concerns.

Committees as a whole should be mission-driven rather than representational. Orlikoff and Totten (1996), two leadership experts, cite the hazards of representational governance on boards of directors: "Board members do not focus on the best interests of the system as a whole, but, rather, focus on the best interests of component parts of the system." In a search committee setting, this problem may be even more insidious. For example, a community politician may be named to a CEO search committee to represent the community, the president of the medical staff is named to represent the medical staff, a minority is named to represent the diverse community, a minister or priest is named to represent the organization's religious foundation, and so forth.

It is quite appropriate to be interested in achieving multiple viewpoints in search committees. However, each member's primary role should be to advance the organization's mission and vision rather than to represent and advance the interests of a specific constituency. During the first meeting, the committee's chair or process leader should initiate a discussion about the potential problems that could occur if members believe their primary role is to represent a specific constituency. Discussing the organization's mission and vision and ensuring that all committee members have a full understanding of these facilitates smoother deliberations later in the process.

Careful thought should be given to committee size. Too large a search committee can be problematic. Committees with no more than nine members but no less than six members tend to perform with greatest efficiency and effectiveness.

Define roles and responsibilities

Search committees and the chair must be clear from the beginning about their role, responsibilities, and authority. They need to know if the committee's function is primarily to screen and recommend candidates or if the committee has actual selection authority. Roles and responsibilities should be defined in writing. An example job description used by one board search committee appears as Appendix 8.1 and a code of ethics developed for search committee members appears as Appendix 8.2 at the end of this chpater.

Clarify the role of those not appointed to the search committee

At times, particularly with a CEO search involving the board of trustees, some board members or other leaders who are not appointed to the search committee feel left out of the decision-making process. Finding ways to appropriately involve them during the process and keep them informed can minimize problems later in the process.

For example, the draft position specification should be sent to all board members for their input. If a search consultant is leading the search, each board member should be given the opportunity to talk privately with the consultant to provide his or her thoughts on the type of person needed for the CEO job. The key here is to involve all board members, even though they may not be members of the search committee. For example, again, following each search committee meeting, a written summary of the committee's activities should be sent to each board member who is not a member of the search committee. Some search committees forward to the full board, for each members' review, detailed minutes of their proceedings and clear records of decision points. In other organizations, the search committee provides a detailed report of its progress during regular board meetings and allows ample opportunity for questions or concerns to be raised. An early expression of concerns ensures that critical issues are not raised during the very delicate final steps of the recruiting process when a finalist has been selected and final negotiations are underway.

Some board search committees offer a standing invitation to all board members to attend search committee meetings. This policy needs to be carefully considered because board members who have not participated in the full search process can disrupt or slow down the process when they join in from time to time. Boards are often large for political reasons. It is not unusual to see boards with 18 to 22 members. To work efficiently, especially on matters as critical as replacing the CEO, the search group should include approximately 6 to 9 individuals. Search committees larger than this begin to display inefficiencies. They have more problems coordinating calendars and reaching compromises. The search process slows down as it becomes harder to make decisions. A CEO candidate wants to know that the search committee was strong and unanimous in its decision. An inefficient committee often sends a signal to a candidate that it is just not certain about the hiring decision. As a result, many strong candidates have been lost.

Finally, the feelings of each board member must be carefully evaluated. Some board members already have feelings of "being on the outside," especially in instances when a strong executive committee makes most of the hard decisions. With larger boards, there may be a feeling that there are two boards—a smaller, executive committee that makes the decisions and the large board that often feels like it simply rubber stamps those decisions.

Board members who are not on the search committee and feel on the outside do not wish to be (and should not be!) embarrassed in community and social settings by apperaing not to know what is going on with a CEO search. This may be even more relevant in a smaller town where the local hospital is a major part of the economy and the community.

Develop a clear process, ground rules and timetable

Working with the chair, the process manager should outline the search committee's process in pursuing its objective. These two individuals should establish the timetable for this process by setting specific dates for

- initial committee meetings to finalize the position specification and review the resumés of the first round of candidates;
- first and follow-up interviews; and
- meetings to evaluate finalists, review recommendations, and make selection decisions, as appropriate.

Committee members should come to the first meeting prepared to set calendar dates and meet the action steps of a clearly delineated process and timetable. Presetting dates for critical activities early in the process greatly enhances the likelihood that all committees members will be able to fully participate in all aspects of the search. A sample CEO search plan appears as Figure 8.1.

Ground rules should be discussed and established early in the process. Many search committees find themselves in the final stages of a selection process spending an inordinate amount of time debating the *hows* and *whys* of the process. At times, search committees spend hours late in the search process debating whether or not they should conduct secret ballot votes on finalist candidates, whether they should use a written ranking sheet to pick the finalist, or even who will cast votes. In some cases, a search committee member may think that it is acceptable to send someone to vote for him or her by proxy.

Figure 8.1 Sample CEO Search Plan and Schedule

- First meeting of search committee: September 3, 2001.
- Evaluate search firms and chose one to work with organization: September 10, 2001.
- Individual interviews conducted by search firm consultants with board, medical staff, community leaders, hospital staff members, auxiliary, and other key stakeholders: September 17 and 18, 2001.
- Search firm conducts national search and secures five to seven qualified candidates: September 18 through November 1, 2001.
- Search committee conducts interviews with five to seven candidates and selects two preferred candidates: November 1 and 2, 2001.
- Two preferred candidates return for in-depth interviews with a wide range of stakeholders: November 8 and 9, 2001 and November 10 and 11, 2001.
- Search committee meets to select candidate of choice: November 12, 2001.
- Negotiations begin with preferred candidate: November 12, 2001.
- New CEO begins work January 2, 2002.

After the final interviews have been completed, it is critical for the search committee to immediately send a signal to the preferred candidate that indeed, he or she is preferred and the strong consensus choice. Delays may lead the candidate to simply withdraw and say, "Thank you, but this move just is not in the best interest of my family, or my career, or just does not make sense now." If delays are caused by discussions about voting procedures or other matters that should have been decided in advance, the loss is tragic. Hence, early in committee deliberations, agreement should be reached about the voting method, how committee decisions will be made, and other administrative matters.

Manage committee communications

Like what occurs when a new pope is selected in the Catholic Church, many people in a healthcare organization have a high degree of curiosity when a CEO search process is underway. Individuals frequently approach members of the committee to get inside information. Information leaks may become even more prevalent as candidates are interviewed, the search winds down, and word gets out about decision-making proceedings. Search committee communications must be managed appropriately. The distribution to key stakeholders of a plan for the search process, such as the one provided in Figure 8.1, can be helpful to communications management. A communications plan for the search process also can be helpful. The plan outlines the steps of the process, relevant dates, and includes who communicates what, and when that information is communicated.

Providing a plan effectively removes the shroud of secrecy from the search process. People know what the search committee is doing and what to expect. Although the job of the search committee has to be performed in a confidential manner, it also must be done openly within the committee. The committee must be able to deliberate and evaluate without influence from the outside. In the ideal search committee, all members respect each other, discuss openly what is needed and who can do it best, and deliberate candidly and straightforwardly. Do such search committees exist? Too often, communications are not straightforward. At times, search committee members meet in smaller groups surreptitiously outside the meeting. Some committee members campaign inside and outside committee meetings. In such instances, candidates could withdraw because they are able to pick up on what has happened during the search committee process.

Carefully design the interview process

Search committees typically interview each candidate, as a group with all the members present, during a 60- to 90-minute session per candidate. Unfortunately, this approach often favors the candidate who has the best presentation skills, is able to maintain the best eye contact, and is most able to quickly "warm up" to the group. Critical job-based skills directly related to the specific job objectives listed as key tasks for the executive in the first year are often not addressed.

One-on-one interviews and structured group interviews using a list of predeveloped questions can be more effective in eliciting information related to the candidate's skills and experience. For example:

- Describe a situation where your medical staff leadership was in disagreement with your board and detail how you mediated and led the two groups toward agreement.
- Detail the steps you used to merge your hospital with the competitor hospital.
- Describe how you communicated with your board of trustees.
- Describe one of the more difficult situations you have had with key physicians and how you dealt with it.
- Detail how you have developed a closer involvement with community leaders.
- Describe one of the most difficult situations you have had with your employees and how you managed the process.

Committee members should receive as much information as possible about each candidate before the interview. This can reduce the amount of time spent on details that could easily be obtained before the interview.

NEW USES FOR SEARCH COMMITTEES

Search committees are commonly used in healthcare with CEO vacancies, but other new uses have emerged during the past decade. A description of these follows.

Physician executive positions

An increasing number of healthcare CEOs are using search committees to handle preliminary screening for physician executive vacancies. Physician executive search committees give physicians an opportunity to provide input about how the position is defined and the type of candidate that is sought and ultimately selected. They also help physicians to better understand the position's role and authority.

One CEO defined the process of using a physician executive search committee to fill a vice president of medical affairs vacancy as follows:

> The Medical Executive Committee will appoint a search committee comprised of physicians across our medical staff. All major areas and services will be represented. Our search consultant will develop the position specification and a search strategy with input from the search committee. Candidates will be identified by our search consultant, and interviewed by the search committee. The committee will provide the CEO with the names of its top two candidates; the CEO will choose one of these individuals. This process will ensure that the CEO chooses a vice president of medical staff affairs with whom he or she and the physician community can best work.

Clinical and/or nurse executive positions

Many healthcare organizations with academic ties use search committees to handle initial screening of candidates for clinical or nurse executive positions. The "shared governance" approach in contemporary nursing supports use of a search committee to give professional nurses greater input into nursing leadership selection. It must be clear *who* will make the final hiring decision. If this is not clear, the search committee may undermine the process by resisting the final selection or asking for too much involvement in the final decision. A written description such as the one cited earlier can help to provide needed clarity. When used properly, this approach enhances nurse participation in organizational management.

Medical department chairs or section chiefs

Historically in healthcare organizations, medical department chairs and section chiefs were paid only small stipends. The "honor" of performing these roles was passed from individual to individual. That situation has now changed. Increasingly, the positions are full-time ones that provide substantive pay. As a result, selection decisions are much more critical and risky. The "old boys club" approach, with search committee members calling and recruiting friends at other locations, is giving way to a greater involvement of professional search firms and search committees that function as appointed bodies of either the medical executive committee or the board of trustees.

CONCLUDING COMMENTS

Although the complexities involved in their use can often harm a search process, clearly the use of search committees will continue in healthcare. Senior healthcare leaders and board members should ensure that search committees attract the very best talent possible by pursing the strategies described in this chapter.

EVALUATE YOUR ORGANIZATION

1. When our organization uses search committees, the reasons for using a committee approach are clearly understood.

Strongly Disagree	Disagree	Neither Disagree or Agree	Agree	Strongly Agree

2. Search committees always have a strong process manager to ensure proper search management.

Strongly Disagree	Disagree	Neither Disagree or Agree	Agree	Strongly Agree

3. Our search committees have clear charges and the roles and responsibilities are well understood by all members.

Strongly Disagree	Disagree	Neither Disagree or Agree	Agree	Strongly Agree

4. Ground rules, timetables, and key calendar dates are established early in the search process.

Strongly Disagree	Disagree	Neither Disagree or Agree	Agree	Strongly Agree

5. A well-planned and methodical approach to communications is designed to minimize rumor, hearsay, and the perception of conspiracy regarding committee activities.

Strongly Disagree	Disagree	Neither Disagree or Agree	Agree	Strongly Agree

6. Search committee members are expected to be prepared, to be present, and to fully participate in committee activities.

Strongly Disagree	Disagree	Neither Disagree or Agree	Agree	Strongly Agree

7. When needed, committee members are given training in interviewing and selection principles.

Strongly Disagree	Disagree	Neither Disagree or Agree	Agree	Strongly Agree

REFERENCES

Fritsch, S.F. 1992. "Skills for Selecting Leaders." *Health Progress* 34 (9): 42–46.

Orlikoff, J.E., and M.K. Totten. 1996. *The Future of Health Care Governance: Redesigning Boards for a New Era.* Chicago: American Hospital Publishing, Inc., 11.

Sample Search Committee Job Description

Thank you for agreeing to serve on our CEO search committee. The selection of our next CEO may be one of the most important decisions that our board will make during this decade. To ensure your understanding of your responsibilities as a search committee member, we have outlined the following points for your guidance.

1. Committee discussions must be confidential. Pressure is often placed on search committee members to provide updates or progress reports to those outside the committee. Because of the nature of our task, we ask that you refrain from giving any information and suggest a comment similar to:

> We are progressing well and hope to have details available soon. Because of the sensitivity of this issue, we have been asked by the board to avoid divulging any information. I appreciate your understanding of this.

2. We plan to establish all calendar dates at the first committee meeting. We ask that you bring your calendar, work hard with all members to mutually set dates that all can meet, and then strive to attend all of those meetings. While we realize that issues may arise that are unforeseen, your participation is critically important.

3. Your authority as a search committee member is primarily to *recommend* to the full board the preferred final candidate for our CEO position. The full board has the actual final authority to approve that recommendation. Obviously, because the search committee is comprised of a majority of board members and the board chair is serving as the search committee chair, we do not anticipate any problems when the final decision is made.

4. Your full participation in discussions and deliberations is appreciated. While all of our members are strong leaders in their own right, we want all viewpoints and votes to be viewed equally.

5. Please take the time to understand the critical importance of the work that must be done on the front-end preparing for the search. Many view the interview process as the most important part of a search process and do not focus as intently on the development stage. We will ask that you spend significant time considering in detail the precise requirements of our CEO position, the challenging matters that confront him/her, and the types of candidates who would best help us address these matters. We will be spending substantive effort to rather explicitly detail the critical objectives that need to be met in the next 12 to 18 months. We will then define in as much detail as possible the precise characteristics, skills, competencies, experience, and expertise that we will need in a new CEO. This document will serve to help us be more objective in our assessment of candidates as we interview them.

6. The role of our search committee chair is to run the meetings, coordinate matters between and among committee members, and to keep the process moving forward. Our search committee's first task will be to select a search consulting firm to assist us in finding candidates, provide a preliminary screening of candidates, present the best to us, and work with us throughout the process as our search manager.

7. Our time goal is to select the search firm within the next 3 weeks, have the firm begin its work immediately, and review the first candidates eight weeks from that point in time. We will have dates already preset during our first search committee meeting for all of these points as well as first-round interviews with three to four candidates.

Code of Ethics for Search Committee Members

By my signature below, I pledge to adhere to the following:

As a member of the search committee, I accept my responsibility shared by my fellow committee members to protect the integrity of the organization and all prospects, semifinal candidates, and final candidates.

I acknowledge that only the chair of the board of trustees is authorized to speak to the news media on behalf of the board and only the chair of the search committee is authorized to speak to the news media on behalf of the search committee.

I certify that I am not a candidate for the position.

I agree to disclose promptly to the committee any appearance of conflict of interest in a relationship between me and a prospect or candidate.

I acknowledge that information is a crucial component of the search committee's work. This work includes information developed and received about prospects, candidates and their employing organizations. I understand this effort is necessary to attract high-quality finalists, to avoid putting their current positions in jeopardy, and to protect my organization's integrity.

Specifically, I will adhere to the following principles:

- I will respect the absolute confidentiality of all prospects and candidates. I will not reveal the identity of or any other information about prospects and candidates before or after the committee completes its work.
- I will be fair, accurate, honest, and responsible in my management of information germane to the search.
- I will guard against inaccuracies, carelessness, bias, and distortion made by either emphasis or omission of information.
- I will strive to treat issues impartially and handle controversial subjects dispassionately.
- I will give accurate and complete reports on candidates to the search committee chair.
- I will place the best interest of the organization ahead of all special and personal interests and I will use common sense and good judgment in applying ethical principles to search work.
- I will attend all meetings of the search committee and if I am unable to, I will contact the chair in a timely manner.

I consider the letter and spirit of this statement to be a matter of personal responsibility.

Signature   Date

Acknowledgment: With special thanks to Nancy Martin of Witt Kieffer/Educational Management Network.

CHAPTER 9

Executive Search Firms

"As in any outsourcing arrangement, a company that opts to use an executive search firm should proceed with caution. After all, hiring a senior manager is a strategic decision. A company's executives must stay involved every step of the way."

—C. Fernandez-Araoz, 1999

THE HEALTHCARE INDUSTRY has used executive search firms for more than thirty years. Use has greatly increased over the past decade, and is continuing to rise. Experts cite several reasons for this trend. First, some organizations began to experience the leadership talent shortage a number of years ago and are relying on search firms to address the shortage. Second, some leaders indicate that search firms often are able to find and attract candidates that, for whatever reason, the organizations cannot themselves reach. Third, the hectic pace of the healthcare environment requires management attention and focus on the complex issues faced by healthcare organizations. There simply is not enough time for leaders to focus on recruitment. Recruitment at the executive and management level takes a great deal of time, and certainly is more complicated than staff recruitment. Finally, healthcare leaders have begun to realize that the traditional method of recruiting leadership talent—running ads—does not deliver the high-quality results more typical of a focused professional executive search.

Despite increased use of executive search firms, however, few healthcare leaders understand search firms, how they work, and what they do. Because search firm "workings" are still shrouded in mystery, organizations often misuse such firms, resulting in inefficiencies, ineffectiveness, and frustration.

SEARCH FIRM BASICS

To make better use of search firms, healthcare leaders must first acquire a basic knowledge of the types of firms and how they work. Two general types operate in the United States: contingency and retained. Because retained firms are used for the majority of healthcare searches, this chapter focuses on them rather than contingency firms. A brief description of each follows, however, along with a description of common search firm variations.

Contingency firms

A contingency firm focuses on gathering and sending resumés to client organizations. It typically has only a cursory telephone discussion with the candidates it refers, and spends little time getting to know a client organization. Contingency firms function much like a brokerage house. Theirs is a numbers game with primary emphasis on how many resumés can be accumulated and sent to client organizations. Contingency firms charge a fee *only* if the employer hires one of the candidates referred by the firm. Standard fees range from 25 to 33 percent of the first year's compensation of the candidate hired.

Healthcare organizations can employ several contingency firms simultaneously. Although this seems likely to be more efficient than simply working with a single contingency or retained firm, it further reduces the already small incentive for the contingency firm to stay on the job. If the position is difficult to fill or if few candidates can be found, contingency firms will quickly move to other searches that offer a higher probability to "score a hit" and place a candidate. In fact, contingency firm effectiveness is very similar to the effectiveness of newspaper or journal advertisements. Both provide the organization with limited exposure for a short period of time.

Nevertheless, contingency firms are used in healthcare, but mostly for middle-management and supervisory positions. They can also be used when the job is fairly standard and its functions and qualifications are uniform industrywide. Use of contingency firms is also appropriate when there is no hurry to fill the position and the client organization simply wants to review as many resumés as possible. However, when the position requires specialized knowledge and the organization requires in-depth evaluation of candidates' leadership styles and skills, retained firms are the better choice.

Retained firms

Retained firms conduct the majority of higher-level searches in healthcare. They are paid a front-end fee for their services, work exclusively with a client organization, and concentrate extensively on finding a qualified candidate. Retained search engagements contain an element of consulting. Retained search is a much more comprehensive process than simply finding candidates. When done correctly, a retained search offers organizations assistance in evaluating the organization's need for a position as well as more fully developing the position description and thoroughly assessing candidates. Unlike contingency firms, retained firms can be most effective when detailed evaluation and assessment of candidates are needed. Retained firms will expend the effort required for difficult searches. Their traditional fee is one-third of the placement's first-year salary.

The "modus operandi" of a retained firm resembles that of a consultant. At the beginning of the search, retained firm staff meet on-site with client organization leaders to develop the position description, detail the ideal candidate's qualifications and experience, and begin to manage the talent recruitment process. They then identify, screen, and evaluate potential candidates, conduct extensive reference checks, and present acceptable choices to the client organization. Most will also guarantee their placement for some period of time.

Usually when a search firm is retained to conduct the search, the search consultant serves as the process manager, ensuring that an effective and smooth approach is taken. For example, to ensure that a single individual closely manages the CEO search process, the retained firm typically spends significant time working directly with the board and the board search committee. Obviously, the search committee chair should remain closely involved throughout the process.

The work of retained firms frequently continues after the organization hires an executive. Many retained firms spend time on-site following the placement to help ensure the new hire's success. Retained firms are eager to see their placement "stick" because many provide some form of guarantee for the placement. This generally means that if the person leaves within the first year or so, the search firm will conduct another search for a replacement at no cost.

Common variations

Some search firms are "generalist" firms, while others can be described as "specialized" firms. Generalist firms typically are very large firms that conduct searches in all industries; specialized firms typically conduct searches in only one or two industries. The healthcare industry has used both types in the past, although firms specializing in healthcare conduct the majority of searches.

Variations exist in the scope of services provided by some search firms. Some firms are willing to unbundle the various services they offer, charging more like traditional consulting firms for specific pieces of the job. For example, they may assist only in the development of the position specification, or may conduct sourcing to identify candidates for the employer. Or, they may help interview finalist candidates identified by the client organization, conduct reference checks, or evaluate internal candidates.

Variations, of course, exist in the location of search firms. Firms with multiple offices often offer additional value because they can draw candidates beyond the client organization's geographic region. Executives often are willing to relocate or in fact may be seeking relocation.

ENHANCING AND IMPROVING THE USE OF SEARCH FIRMS

Healthcare leaders must be clear about the reasons to use and not to use a search firm. They must define why a search firm is needed or why it is not needed. Search firms can help healthcare leaders by managing the recruiting process, clarifying the position's issues and needs, reducing the time needed for recruiting within the organization, and providing expertise about leadership skills and talent. They also can help broaden the search and broker the final employment arrangements. Healthcare organizations *should not* use search firms if they have qualified recruiting staff and candidates within the organization. To improve the use of search firms, healthcare leaders and search firms must establish reasonable expectations of each other. Detailed information on each topic follows.

Define why a search firm is needed

Healthcare organizations may need a search firm for the following reasons.

1. *To manage the process.* Most healthcare organizations simply are not effective at managing the executive search process and many recognize this fact. Because of other major initiatives, leaders, such as the CEO, COO, or chief human resources officer, may not have the time to devote to a complex and time-consuming search. Some organizations simply do not have the human resources talent or expertise to conduct an executive-level search. Use of a retained search firm can ensure that the search proceeds and is concluded in a timely manner. Expertise offered by the firm often enhances the search's efficiency.

2. *To clarify issues and needs.* Often, no clear-cut consensus exists within an organization about the need for the position or its responsibilities. Occasionally, there is conflict about the characteristics and experience required of candidates. Highly effective retained search firms are able to clarify or frame these issues. Because they are not a part of the organization's political environment, they can identify key issues "lurking beneath the table" that need to be discussed by the senior leadership group. They can offer their client information about best practices and how other organizations have approached similar issues.

3. *To provide expertise.* Many retained search firms are expert at interviewing and evaluating leadership talent. Because they spend so much time with these activities, they have developed a large database with which to compare candidates and make experienced judgments. This capability extends beyond that possible for many senior leaders. If performed correctly, the search firm's evaluations provide significant insights about candidates' abilities. This increases the probability that

the selected candidate will be successful. Ultimately, the expertise offered by search firms may be the most convincing argument for their use. High-quality hiring decisions are critical to an organization's success. Search firms also can provide significant expertise in other aspects of the search process, such as defining job responsibilities and authority, setting an appropriate compensation range, developing employment contracts, and using evaluation and assessment tools.

4. *To broaden the search.* Using a search firm typically ensures the casting of a broader net for candidates. As a search firm conducts its sourcing work, the size of the candidate pool increases, which enhances the likelihood of achieving a best-fit hire. This often is another of the most compelling reasons to use a search firm. A retained search firm with multiple offices around the nation can identify a greater number of candidates than one with a single office.

5. *To provide objectivity.* Search firms often provide more objectivity than can be achieved through other search approaches. Because they are not part of the organizations they serve, retained search firms offer impartial evaluations of both internal and external candidates and more targeted and objective assistance in defining issues and barriers to an effective search.

6. *To mediate or broker final employment arrangements.* Retained search firms can serve in an advisory or mediating capacity in brokering employment arrangements with the final candidate. In doing so, they provide a valuable buffer between the organization and candidate during discussions about delicate and sensitive compensation matters. As a middleman, a search firm can keep the negotiations moving positively and unemotionally toward conclusion.

7. *To handle an important search when the organization's leaders do not have the time to do so.* Often, the time constraints of an executive search become one of the prime reasons to use a

search firm. Busy executives will use a firm as an "extender" if they are involved with key projects. At times, multiple vacancies exist and search firms complement internal resources in filling leadership openings quickly.

Define why a search firm is not needed

Healthcare organizations must be very clear about why a search firm is *not* needed, if this is the case. A description of common reasons follows.

1. *The organization attracts talent without having to seek it out.* Some organizations are nationally renowned and their reputations serve as a built-in magnet for leadership talent. Because the organization is viewed as a desirable place to work, they receive unsolicited resumés from very talented leaders and attract widespread attention when they do have an open position.

2. *Internal talent is available to conduct a successful search.* Some organizations have talented human resources executives or others who have the time and expertise to manage a leadership search process. Human resource executives in larger organizations may be knowledgeable enough about the nuances of effective search processes to manage the search as effectively as search firms.

3. *Highly qualified internal candidates are present and can fill the job.* The organization may be blessed with highly qualified internal candidates. If the organization has such candidates, is committed to promoting from within, and has a clear succession plan, there is little reason for it to engage in an outside search. However, some organizations will still retain a search firm to conduct an external search to better justify selection of the internal candidate and validate the overall search process.

Select a search firm

To select the best possible search firm, a healthcare organization should ask and answer the following questions.

- *What type of expertise is needed to conduct the search?*
  Organizations should consider the background of the search consultant. Does this individual fully understand healthcare? As mentioned earlier, generalist search consultants may not yield as good results as a search consultant with experience in the healthcare field. Search consultants who have worked in executive positions in healthcare often bring a deeper understanding of the position's needs. For example, a search consultant who has worked in an academic medical center may have a better understanding of how to conduct a search in that area. A chief information officer search might be best handled by a search consultant who has previously worked as a CIO in healthcare.
- *How well does the search consultant understand the organization?*
  One of the more important aspects in choosing a search consultant is evaluating his or her knowledge and understanding of the hiring organization. Ongoing relationships with the same search consultant can help the consultant gain deep knowledge about the organization, becoming, in effect, more of a "partner" in the organization's vision and strategy. Some search consultants develop long-term relationships with certain healthcare organizations and handle all of their search work.
- *Will the consultant we choose be the person who will do the work?*
  Although the answer to this may seem evident, some search firms use a number of "backroom" consultants to handle parts of a search assignment. These individuals may or may not be qualified to represent the organization, and they may not be as effective in getting the attention of qualified candidates. Before choosing a search consultant, the organization

and consultant should reach a clear understanding about who will be handling which parts of the search.

- *What is the search consultant's and firm's reputation?* Healthcare organizations may want to check references of other organizations that have used the firm or the particular search consultant they are evaluating. They may also wish to review with the consultant the specific searches that he or she recently conducted.

- *Does the search consultant have the time to devote to the search?* The search industry can be a cyclical business, where search consultants are busier at certain times. The organization should ask the search consultant about his or her present search load and ability to dedicate focused time to the organization's search.

- *What skills does the search firm or the search consultant bring to the evaluation of candidates? How does he or she evaluate candidates?* Although these questions may seem to be a given in the search industry, it is critical for the organization to assess the consultant's and firm's expertise in the evaluation process. Perhaps the single most important measure of success in the search industry is a successful hire. The organization should probe what a search consultant does to ensure that no hiring mistake is made and how he or she defines a successful hire. Leaders should ask how candidates are evaluated and understand the process used by the consultant for interviewing and assessing candidates.

- *Can and will the firm or the individual consultant provide full consultation?* Retained searches usually involve more than simply "order taking." The search consultant should have the expertise to provide general consulting and counsel. Search consultants who know the industry well, through actually having worked in the industry or gaining experience through the years, can provide a definitive difference in conducting a search. A search consultant who has been a CEO in the past can provide valuable insight as could others who have served in executive positions.

- *Does the search firm or the search consultant bring any additional expertise or knowledge?* The firm or consultant selected also may have expertise beyond the traditional search industry. For example, they may be able to provide in-depth assistance in compensation evaluation. Although they are not compensation consulting firms, search firms do have access to some of the best compensation data available and can use this information to help an organization better assess the appropriate salary level of open positions. The search consultant with past consulting or executive experience may also bring specialized knowledge of particular areas of the organization, such as strategic planning, marketing, and conducting leadership retreats.

Feedback from executive decision-makers can be used to build a helpful checklist for evaluating executive search services for your organization. Based upon the "top ten" attributes in order of importance, Figure 9.1 offers ten areas to explore with your prospective executive search partner. Armed with answers to these questions, an organization's leaders will be well-equipped to make an informed decision about the best possible search firm or search consultant.

Establish reasonable expectations

When a healthcare organization retains a search firm to conduct an executive search, both the organization and search firm must have and meet reasonable expectations.

It is reasonable to expect a retained search firm to do the following:

- Detail the scope of services to be provided, professional fee arrangement, expenses, cancellation policy, and guarantees.

Figure 9.1 Checklist for Evaluating Executive Search Services

1. What is the search firm's candidate screening process, and how are quality control measures built into it? How are reference checks conducted?
2. Does the search consultant provide ongoing and meaningful communication throughout the process? Are you kept apprised of progress and problems?
3. What kind of rapport are you seeking from the search consultant? Does he or she appear interested in building a strategic business relationship?
4. What kind of experience does the search firm have in your industry? Is their experience directly applicable to your needs?
5. What is the search firm's record of similar placements? How do they demonstrate their success?
6. Have you or a colleague worked with this search firm previously? Was it a positive experience?
7. Can the search firm help you establish aggressive but realistic deadlines? Do they meet those deadlines?
8. Does the search firm have national reach with access to a broad pool of candidates? What kind of database do they use to achieve this reach?
9. Does the search firm have an intimate understanding of your organization? Do they actively pursue a greater understanding of your leadership needs?
10. What is the search firm's reputation? What strengths do they have? Do your colleagues recommend them?

Source: Web site: www.wittkieffer.com. Used with permission.

- Spend significant time getting to know and understand the client organization, the position to be filled, and the community. This involves visiting the client, meeting with various leaders and stakeholders, and learning about the organization's culture and practices.
- Clarify the qualifications needed to fill the job. Key position objectives and the attributes of preferred candidates must be

explicit. The best firms develop detailed position specifications to ensure complete agreement with the client organization on the requirements of the position. Once approved, they use this as a marketing document to attract potential candidates.

- Establish specific time guidelines for the search process. Dates for progress updates and presentation of candidates should be set well in advance.
- Represent the client organization's interests. The search firm should provide complete and unambiguous representation for its client. For example, the search firm should not withhold pertinent information about candidates.
- Properly screen and thoroughly evaluate all candidates and present only those who meet the requirements of the position. Open discussions between the search firm and client organization about the candidates and their qualifications and background are essential.
- Maintain professional contact with candidates, treating them with respect at all times.
- Fully disclose any barriers to an effective search, such as salary level, expectations of the position, or location or reputation of the organization.
- Maintain confidentiality of organizational information gained during the search process. In addition, search firms must use information gleaned from candidates solely for the search's presentations. The confidentiality of such information must be maintained.
- Behave ethically and conscientiously by honoring confidences.

It is reasonable to expect a client healthcare organization to do the following:

- Spend ample time with the search firm as the search process commences. Successful searches are much more than order taking. Healthcare leaders should be prepared for meetings with the search consultant and provide as much detail about the position as possible. Spending front-end time with search firm staff ensures a full and mutual understanding of the position. This is critical to search process success.

- Provide honest and detailed information about the organization. The search firm and client organization must develop a relationship of trust. Trust is a two-way street. Problems and concerns should be identified by both parties. For example, the search firm needs to know the truth about the issues surrounding the departure of the incumbent and the organization's financial condition. Similarly, the search firm needs confidential strategic or other data and facts relevant to the search. The healthcare organization needs truthful information about each candidate. Leaders and search firms should provide this information up front to avoid worst-case scenarios, such as occurs when finalist candidates raise relevant information about which the search firm or organization is unaware when negotiating final employment arrangements or, worse yet, in their first few days on the job.

- Provide as much detail as possible when rejecting one of the search firm's recommended candidates. This helps the search firm better understand fit and qualifications and keeps the search on target.

- Respond to search firm communication in a timely manner. This is particularly important during delicate, end-of-search discussions with final candidates. Many good candidates have changed their minds about joining an organization because the organization responded slowly to their questions or requests.

- Ensure that candidates receive respectful treatment when interviewing with organization staff. Remember, that in a time of leadership talent shortages, the interview should help market and sell the organization and position.

- Follow all appropriate fair practices employment laws. This means ensuring that all interviewers ask only legally appropriate questions and behave professionally.

CONCLUDING COMMENTS

During the next decades of leadership talent shortage, the use of search firms is likely to continue its decade-long climb. Successful healthcare organizations will gain in-depth understanding of why and how best to use such firms. Readers interested in learning more about search firms may wish to consult the web sites of firms that provide information on the search industry, such as Kennedy Information Inc. (www.kennedyinfo.com) and Hunt-Scanlon Corporation (www.hunt-scanlon.com). Readers may also want to visit the web sites of several search firms such as www.wittkieffer.com, www.heidrick.com, www.kornferry.com, and www.spencerstuart.com.

EVALUATE YOUR ORGANIZATION

1. Those in charge of recruiting managers and executives in our organization are well versed on search firms and how they operate.

Strongly Disagree	Disagree	Neither Disagree or Agree	Agree	Strongly Agree

2. When our organization uses a search firm, we provide the search consultants with sufficient background and information on our needs.

Strongly Disagree	Disagree	Neither Disagree or Agree	Agree	Strongly Agree

3. When a search firm is used, the expectations of both parties are clearly discussed and agreed to.

Strongly Disagree	Disagree	Neither Disagree or Agree	Agree	Strongly Agree

4. The need for confidentiality is understood by all parties in a search process.

Strongly Disagree	Disagree	Neither Disagree or Agree	Agree	Strongly Agree

5. When working with a search firm, we strive for a strong partnership.

Strongly Disagree	Disagree	Neither Disagree or Agree	Agree	Strongly Agree

6. When working with a search firm, we maintain close and frequent communications.

Strongly Disagree	Disagree	Neither Disagree or Agree	Agree	Strongly Agree

7. When working with a search firm, both the firm and our organization follow all fair employment laws.

Strongly Disagree	Disagree	Neither Disagree or Agree	Agree	Strongly Agree

8. When rejecting candidates, we provide the search firm with a comprehensive understanding of the reasons for the rejection.

Strongly Disagree	Disagree	Neither Disagree or Agree	Agree	Strongly Agree

REFERENCE

Fernandez-Araoz. C. 1999. "Hiring Without Firing." *Harvard Business Review* 77 (4): 115.

CHAPTER 10

Assessments and Assessment Psychologists

"There is an understandable tendency to attribute monstrous deeds accompanied by callousness, remorselessness, lying, and failure to accept responsibility to a monstrous nature. This attributional tendency leaves one in mute incomprehension of how ordinary people, as well as respected leaders, can coldly perpetrate atrocities—as they regularly do—under a variety of circumstances and incentives."

—M. K. Levenson, K. Kiehl, and C. Fitzpatrick, 1995

HIRING THE RIGHT executives is one of the most important decisions an organization will make, yet this is not always an easy task. This chapter will make five points. First, the decision to hire a healthcare executive is too important to rely solely on the outcome of an interview process. Healthcare organizations must commit to using other assessments to clarify and resolve issues that surround interview results. Second, measuring executive talent is difficult because a systematic definition of performance dimensions associated with executive success simply does not exist. Third, the assessment industry is huge and unregulated, with more than 2,600 assessment test publishers in the United States alone. The quality of assessments, what they are designed to do, and how

This chapter was written by Jared D. Lock, Ph.D., manager of business development for Hogan Assessment Systems.

they are used vary greatly. Fourth, when an organization decides to use assessments, the organization should address several issues to ensure the appropriate use of high-quality assessments. Finally, executive selection psychologists can help organizations assess and hire executive talent. Such psychologists work, however, in an unregulated market. How they conduct business, their background, and the quality of their services vary widely. The purpose of this chapter is to give an organization the upper edge when using assessments or psychologist assessment services.

WHAT IS AN ASSESSMENT?

Many organizations need to better understand what constitutes an assessment. Most organizations view only paper and pencil tests as assessments. However, interviews and resumé screens also are assessments. According to the *Uniform Guidelines on Employee Selection Procedures*, in layman terms, an assessment is any procedure an organization uses to make a decision concerning a person's suitability for the job (EEOC 1978). Hence, when an organization screens thirty resumés and selects five candidates to interview, they have used an assessment. When a hiring manager interviews five candidates and selects one, he or she has used an assessment. The difference between these assessments and a test is that the interview and resumé screen usually are not structured, cannot be validated in a statistical sense, and may cause organizational problems should a lawsuit arise.

WHY NOT JUST INTERVIEW EXECUTIVE CANDIDATES?

Why should organizations worry about executive assessment beyond the traditional interview? Consider the following points.

- Poor leadership performance is a widespread problem. At least one out of every two leaders is not performing up to expected levels (Shipper and Wilson 1991). Such failure of a seemingly able executive is referred to as "derailing." Executives who are derailing often also have good social skills and apparent potential, which makes it difficult to measure dysfunctional characteristics in an employment interview (Mowday 1978; Sarbin 1954).

- The literature about executive derailment shows quite convincingly that within the population of bright and charismatic potential leaders, who interview well, a substantial proportion will fail due to overwhelming personality defects (Bentz 1985; Harris and Hogan 1992; Hogan 1994). Some estimate this proportion to be up to 75 percent (Levenson, Kiehl, and Fitzpatrick 1995). Furthermore, these defects are rarely visible to a hiring organization's board of directors until *after* a leader has been hired or promoted.

- Hiring a bad executive will cost, on average, at least three times the executive's base pay plus bonus. Given the large salaries of healthcare executives, making the right selection decision assumes critical financial importance.

- In studying leadership and executive derailment, research study authors Hogan and Roberts (2000) conclude that:
  - Dysfunctional dispositions are associated with poor executive leadership;
  - These characteristics coexist with excellent interpersonal skills;
  - Most businesses try to reduce employment costs by screening hourly employees, instead of hiring the right executives; and
  - Executives with dysfunctional dispositions do not learn from their mistakes and erode the trust and confidence of those who work for them.

- Executives are changing jobs and industries more frequently, sometimes making "radical career changes" into new fields

(Perosa and Perosa 1997). An interview based on technical competence (i.e., how well the person understands the industry) may unfairly disqualify an excellent candidate.

- High-quality organizations and executive job seekers each focus their employment decision heavily on executive-environment fit, defined as the congruence between the job seeker's and organization's values and vision (Carson and Carson 1998; Carson and Mowsesian 1993; Meir 1995; Meir, Hadas and Noyfeld 1997; Meir, Tziner, and Glazner 1997). Few organizations, however, have a ready measure of organizational fit.

More than ever before, healthcare organizations should ensure that an executive candidate meets the organization's technical, personal, and organizational requirements. Assessments provide this objective evaluation of a job seeker's qualities and characteristics. Nonetheless, many healthcare organizations continue to rely on interviews and the gut-feel of the hiring team and/or board of directors.

WHAT SHOULD BE MEASURED WHEN ASSESSING EXECUTIVES?

As organizations embrace assessments in their selection processes, the first question that arises is, What should be measured? According to Hogan (Goleman 1990), "[One of the worst problems in industry is] the failure of executives to advance the interests of their companies." *Executive leadership* is defined as the ability to get others to put aside their own self-interests to pursue the interests of the group, department, or company. This definition reflects both motivation in a general sense and specific motivation toward common organizational goals. Good executive leaders will not simply motivate their employees, but motivate them toward goals that lead to desired organizational outcomes.

When determining what to measure in evaluating job seekers, organizations should consider the following four job performance classifications: technical fit, personal fit, leadership fit/derailment potential, and organizational fit.

Technical fit

Technical fit is the most widely recognized aspect of job performance and forms the basis of most skills assessments (Campbell 1992), abilities, aptitudes (U.S. Department of Defense 1984), and knowledge. Most hiring managers will focus their interview efforts on technical fit. It is very important to make sure that the person to be hired is able to (a) effectively perform the tasks and duties of the job; and/or (b) learn how to do the tasks and activities relatively quickly. When hiring a new tax accountant or healthcare executive, the organization hopes that the new hire understands the tax code or, in the case of the executive, the healthcare industry. The technical fit of candidates should continue to be assessed. However, assessment must be expanded to include the next three categories of "fit-ness" as well.

Personal fit

This category is based on measures of normal personality (Hogan and Hogan 1995). Such measures indicate how a person will interact in the workplace, if the person is motivated to do a good job, and how well that person will get along with others. Most technical fit interviews and measures will indicate *if* a person can do a job. In contrast, personal fit measures provide information concerning *how* a person will perform, including the person's ability to get along with others and to perform under stress. They also will provide information on his or her level of interest in learning and expanding current capabilities. For example, a good measure of personal fit will help the organization understand if the job seeker actually wants to manage other people and how the job seeker will approach the leadership function.

Personal fit can be evaluated using most high-quality measures of normal personality. The relationship between high-quality personal fit measures and potential job performance is very strong (Barrick and Mount 1991; Hogan and Holland 2000; Schmidt and Hunter 1998) and can be used to determine if the job seeker will approach the job in a manner that is consistent with the organization's expectations.

Leadership fit/derailment potential

The leadership fit/derailment potential category is largely overlooked by organizations because few assessments exist in this area and this type of fit is difficult to measure through traditional interviews. Leadership fit/derailment potential focuses not on those characteristics that show up under normal conditions, but instead on those characteristics that show up under stressful conditions, conditions of uncertainty, and novel situations. While assessment of personal fit is interested in those *positive* characteristics associated with leader success, the assessment of leadership fit/derailment potential is concerned with the *negative* behaviors associated with leader failure or derailment. A well-validated measure of leadership fit/derailment potential (Hogan and Hogan 1997) can be used to predict many job-related behaviors associated with management success and failure (Bentz 1985; Lock 1996).

Two points about measures of leadership fit/derailment potential warrant mention. First, these measures should be used in conjunction with technical and personal fit measures to provide a comprehensive understanding of both positive and negative leadership characteristics. Second, interviews rarely, if ever, detect the negative characteristics associated with leadership derailment. Hence, measuring these characteristics is critical.

Organizational fit

Organizational fit is a budding and unique area of executive selection assessment. It is based on the premise that it is important for job seekers and healthcare organization to share similar values and be motivated by similar goals. The relationship between shared values, employee performance, satisfaction, and retention have been well documented (Lock and Thomas 1998). Because leadership turnover is extremely expensive, healthcare organizations should understand that it is far easier to recruit and retain leaders whose values fit those of the organization than to change the organization to meet the leader's views. Organizational fit measures assess those characteristics that are known to be associated with enhanced performance (Borman and Motowidlo 1993).

Two points about organizational fit measures should be mentioned here. First, these measures do not indicate how well a leader performs but how well a leader *will* perform given an organization's culture, values, and motivations. Second, organizational fit measures provide the board of directors with an understanding of how to motivate the leader. This can facilitate the achievement of long-term performance improvement goals.

WHAT ARE THE TYPES OF ASSESSMENTS?

Although there are many different ways to classify assessments, a broad interpretation of five assessment types follows.

Technical assessments

Technical assessments determine if the executive has the skills to do the job. These assessments include background and reference checks, resumé screens, degree qualifications, management interviews, and biographical data questionnaires. The main goal is to determine if the person has the background to perform the functions of the job with little intervention.

Interviews

Interviews are face-to-face interactions between the job seeker and an organizational representative. They are designed to help the organization learn more about the job seeker by asking a series of questions to evaluate how well the job seeker would perform in the job. Interviews can be both unstructured and structured and are the main form of assessment used by organizations, although the validity of interviews has been called seriously into question (Avery and Champion 1982; Hunter and Hunter 1984).

Simulations

The purpose of simulations is to extrapolate how a job seeker will perform in the work environment based on how well the job seeker performs in a simulated executive environment. Simulations can include interactions with potential future coworkers, public presentations, report writing, and "in-basket" exercises. An in-basket exercise involves asking an executive to review a stack of memos, letters, reports, and other information as if he or she had been out of the office for some time. The executive is expected to respond in an appropriate fashion to requests and urgent needs. Simulations are popular because they are face valid (i.e., they look like the job). However, they are costly to develop and operate and are very time consuming.

Personality assessments

Personality assessments provide information about how a person will respond to his or her work and organizational environment.

Personality assessments in general are difficult to fake, show no evidence of adverse impact (such as legal issues), and can provide high-quality information concerning a person's reputation. The main criticism is that the questions are not specific to the job, and therefore such assessments are not face valid.

Cognitive ability assessments

Cognitive ability assessments measure how a person will respond to the job in a cognitive manner. They are used to determine such things as a job seeker's judgment, problem-solving ability, decision-making capacity, abstract thinking, technical thinking, and in some cases, creativity. Cognitive ability assessments show a high correlation with job performance but also result in adverse impact against protected minority groups.

DO WE REALLY WANT TO USE ASSESSMENTS? IF SO, WHICH ONE(S)?

Many organizations are wary of assessments because they place restrictions on the selection decision ("The test said I could not hire you"), can be difficult to understand ("What does skydiving have to do with being an accountant"), and stifle the use of gut-feel ("I know a good employee when I see one"). We view assessments as a third-party review of the job seeker's fit with the position and the organization. After the interviews are completed, an assessment provides an objective opinion. This often is critical to making a good-fit hiring decision and is highly recommended.

When choosing assessments, an organization should concentrate on one key criterion: Can the assessment activities predict future job performance and/or satisfaction in some statistical sense? In other words, does the assessment have validity? *Validity* is simply the ability to predict nontest outcomes like job performance.

Many common assessments, such as the Myers-Briggs Type Indicator (MBTI), are not able to predict job performance or executive effectiveness, and hence do not have validity. In fact, even though the MBTI manual specifically states that there is no evidence that the MBTI predicts job performance or executive effectiveness (Myers et al. 1998), many consultants, psychologists, and organizations use the MBTI erroneously as a pre-employment selection assessment tool.

Many organizations are starting to use psychological evaluations and assessment procedures. However, "Many business people see psychological assessment as a cottage industry with no barriers to entry. They believe issues of reliability and validity are the wonkish concerns of psychonerds, rather than the heart and soul of assessment" (Lock and Hogan 2000). With so many test publishers in the United States alone, deciding where and how to use an executive assessment can be overwhelming. Most business people do not understand that research should be conducted on an assessment to verify that it is valid and reliable. A car-buying metaphor can help illustrate this. Although the engine's reliability and validity are the most important features of a new car, few people ask questions about and make a choice based on the engine. Instead, they choose cars based on color and upholstery design ("I like the way this assessment looks").

Assessments (and assessment psychologists, described later in the chapter) are not perfect, and some are better than others. Organizations need to evaluate the ability of assessments to predict future job performance. A simple model for evaluating assessments includes four factors described here: past history of success; impact based on gender, race, or age; intended use; and implementation strategy. Each of these factors should be addressed by the test publisher and by any assessment psychologist who has recommended or is being asked to recommend executive candidates.

Past history of success

The assessment should have a documented history of success in predicting job performance. Underlying this statement is the concept of validity described earlier. The great majority of assessments have no record or understanding of validity. If the assessment does not have a well-documented history with assessment scores that have been correlated with job performance measures, the assessment should not be used. Many assessments have a successful history of measuring job performance. A healthcare organization hiring high-level executives should not have to be a guinea pig for a test publisher with no evidence of assessment validity.

No history of gender, race, or age differences

People of different race, gender, and age should not score differently on an assessment based on their race, gender, or age. Differential scoring based on these factors can create serious legal troubles for an organization if a job seeker who is denied a job files a lawsuit against the organization. Most cognitive ability measures produce different scoring patterns based on gender and race, while personality measures do not. Under the law, in instances of adverse impact against protected minorities, the organization must perform specific activities to effectively and legally use the assessment.

Intended use as a selection instrument

Some assessments were developed to be used as career guidance tools, for personal development, for team building, or for selection. Although spoons and knives are both silverware, one would not use a spoon to cut a steak. In a similar vein, assessments should be used for their intended purpose *only*. For example, as described earlier and as specified in its manual, the MBTI should not be used as a selection tool.

Clear implementation strategy

Obtaining an assessment is the first step; determining how to use it is the second. In general, most assessment test publishers are good at researching their assessments but are poor implementers. When discussing possible use of an assessment, the organization should ask the following questions.

- How will the test publisher determine a company or job profile? How much time will this take? What is the cost associated with the profiling activities? Organizations should be wary of an assessment that can be implemented without tailoring it specifically to the organization.
- What are the scoring and reporting options? Test publishers should provide the assessment options desired by organizations, including paper and pencil, software-based, and Internet-based tests. Also, the publisher should offer different reports based on different needs, for example, selection, development, management, and so forth.
- What is the assessment's "normative population" against which other scores are compared? What are the relevant characteristics of that population? Is the population representative of the organization's industry or of the job in question? Assessments with a clear history of use in the workplace should be used rather than those without a normative population or those with an off-target population, such as undergraduate psychology students.

The answers to these questions let an organization evaluate an assessment's worth. However, this represents a substantial amount of information for an organization to collect. Some organizations may not have the resources or time, especially if they are only hiring one executive. Lacking time and expertise, many organizations turn to psychologists to help them with their selection process.

HOW DO WE SELECT A GOOD EXECUTIVE ASSESSMENT PSYCHOLOGIST?

Executive assessment by psychologists is a growing field. Many independent psychologists as well as large consulting firms offer services providing psychological evaluations of executive candidates. This reflects, in part perhaps, the reduction in federal money and benefits for the psychological community as well as business demands. Prior to hiring a psychologist to assist with executive selection, organizations should consider his or her credentials and past performance. A description of each follows.

Credentials

Not all psychologists are created alike. Different schools focus on different psychological theories and practices. Some are very practical; others are very theoretical. Some are very business-like or applied and some are very academic. An individual can earn a psychologist degree through, among others, school, counseling, industrial/organizational, clinical, and social psychology programs.

Prior to choosing a psychologist, at a minimum the organization should address the following issues related to credentials.

- Does the psychologist have a basic background in assessment for job selection? Programs in industrial/organizational psychology provide the required basic background. Clinical experience is not considered experience in executive selection.
- If not an industrial/organizational psychologist, has the

individual received proper training within the field of executive selection assessment?

- Are references available with whom to discuss the psychologist's credentials and success?

At the very least, all psychologists who perform executive assessment activities should be concerned with or have a basic understanding of:

- Job analysis—how to identify the performance dimensions associated with success.
- Assessment selection—how to link these performance dimensions to available assessments.
- Implementation strategy—how to create a profile and the process that each applicant will go through.
- Candidate selection—how to determine the best candidate.

Quality of services

Psychologists do not all provide the same level of customer service or product quality. Much like every other job in the world, some executive assessment psychologists are high performers and some are low performers. Some provide services that are on target to meet the organization's specific needs; others do not. Hence, organizations must assess the psychologist and the services to be provided. Three factors will help an organization discern whether the psychologist is likely to perform at expected levels.

The first factor is answered by the question, Who will be doing the work and will the work be on target? Many large consulting firms use non-psychologist ghostwriters to compose the first draft of an executive assessment report. The report then is reviewed by a psychologist and finalized. Organizations should inquire about who will be doing the assessment work and if such individuals are certified and have the appropriate degrees. The organization should evaluate whether the consulting firm is charging an appropriate amount based on who is doing the work. Evaluation of the nature of the services to be provided is also needed. How will the psychologist formulate a plan for identifying an appropriate profile for the job in question? Is the psychologist using assessments that were designed for use in workplace settings, or are the assessments meant to be used with clinical populations?

Second, the psychologist to be retained for executive assessment and search should link his or her proposed assessment "battery" to the four fit areas described earlier (technical, personal, leadership/derailment, and organization fit). If gaps in measurement exist, for example there is no leadership/derailment measure, the psychologist's practices and procedures should be questioned. Also, the quality of the assessment for each area should be evaluated to ensure proper coverage of the performance dimension.

Third and finally, the organization and psychologist should agree on and outline the specific steps to be followed when hiring an executive. Once both parties agree on the assessment and selection process, the *same* process should be followed for *all* candidates. This is important to both the organization and the psychologist. Adding extra assessments to one applicant's battery or conducting team interviews with one but not all applicants is a serious issue that can create significant legal troubles for an organization.

CONCLUDING COMMENTS

Hiring executives is one of the biggest decisions organization leaders make and assessments are an important part of the executive selection process. Although most organization leaders are not psychological assessment experts, they can become familiar with the process and the questions to ask to determine which assessments or psychologists to use. Guidelines presented in this chapter should facilitate this process.

There are legal implications with using assessments. These relate to treating people fairly. The two biggest issues associated with selection assessment systems are consistency and adverse impact—the extent to which people of different race, age, or gender score differently. When at all possible, organizations should use assessments that do not have a history of adverse impact on protected minority groups. They also should ensure use of the same selection process with all candidates.

Executive selection procedures should focus on whole job performance. Technical fit, personal fit, leadership fit/derailment potential, and organizational fit are each important. A basic understanding of how the executive selection system measures these performance domains should facilitate positive hiring decisions.

Finally, make sure the psychologist used by the organization for assessing executives is certified and trained to work in organizational settings.

REFERENCES

Arvey, R., and J. Campion. 1982. "The Employment Interview: A Survey and Review of Recent Research." *Personnel Psychology* 35: 281–322.

Barrick, M., and M. Mount. 1991. "The Big-Five Personality Dimensions and Job Performance: A Meta-Analysis." *Personnel Psychology* 44: 1–26.

Borman, W., and S. Motowidlo. 1993. "Expanding the Criterion Domain to Include Elements of Contextual Performance." In *Personnel Selection in Organizations*, edited by N. Schmitt, W. Borman, and Associates. San Francisco: Jossey-Bass.

Bentz, J. 1985. "A View from the Top: A 30-Year Perspective of Research Devoted to the Discovery, Description, and Prediction of Extreme Behavior." Paper presented at the annual meeting of the American Psychological Association, Los Angeles.

Campbell, D. 1992. *Campbell Interest and Skills Survey*. National Computer Systems: Minneapolis, MN.

Carson, A. and P. Carson. 1998. "Career Commitment, Competencies, and Citizenship." *Journal of Career Assessment* 6 (2): 23–27.

Carson, A., and R. Mowsesian. 1993. "Moderators of the Prediction of Job Satisfaction from Congruence: A Test of Holland's Theory." *Journal of Career Assessment* 1(2): 52–59.

Equal Employment Opportunity Commission (EEOC). 1978. *Uniform Guidelines on Employee Selection Procedures.* Federal Register 43: 382990-38315.

Goleman, D. 1990. "The Dark Side of Charisma. *The New York Times,* April 1, Section 3, Part 2.

Harris, G., and J. Hogan. 1992. "Perceptions and Personality Correlates of Managerial Effectiveness." Paper presented at the 13th Annual Psychology in the Department of Defense Symposium, Colorado Springs, CO, April.

Hogan, R. 1994 "Trouble at the Top: Causes and Consequences of Managerial Incompetence." *Consulting Psychology Journal* 46 (1): 9–15.

Hogan, R., and J. Hogan. 1995. *The Hogan Personality Inventory.* Tulsa, OK: Hogan Assessment Systems.

Hogan, R., and J. Hogan. 1997. *The Hogan Development Survey.* Tulsa, OK: Hogan Assessment Systems.

Hogan, J., and B. Holland. 2000. "Examining Personality Links to Work Motives for Getting Along and Getting Ahead." Paper presented at the annual meeting of the Society for Industrial and Organizational Psychology, New Orleans, LA.

Hogan, R., and B. Roberts. 2000. "A Socioanalytic Perspective on Person-Environment Interaction." In *Person-Environment Psychology* 2nd ed., edited by W. Walsh, K. Craik, and R. Price. Mahwah, NJ: Lawrence Earlbaum Associates.

Hunter, J., and R. Hunter. 1984. Validity and Utility of Alternate Predictors of Job Performance." *Psychological Bulletin* 18 (98): 72–98.

Levenson, M., K. Kiehl, and C. Fitzpatrick. 1995. "Assessing Psychopathic Attributes in a Non-institutionalized Population." *Journal of Personality and Social Psychology* 68 (1): 151–158.

Lock, J. 1996. "Developiing an Integrative Model of Leadership." Unpublished doctoral dissertation. Tulsa, OK: University of Tulsa.

Lock, J., and R. Hogan. 2000. "Expanding the Focus of Career Assessment." *Journal of Career Assessment* 3 (4): 13–17.

Lock, J., and L. Thomas. 1998. "The Effects of Leaders' Values on Group Citizenship." Poster presented at the annual meeting of the Society for Industrial and Organizational Psychology, Dallas, TX, April.

Meir, E. 1995. "Elaboration of the Relation Between Interest Congruence and Satisfaction." *Journal of Career Assessment* 3 (3): 31–35.

Meir, E., C. Hadas, and M. Noyfeld. 1997. "Person-Environment Fit in Small Army Units." *Journal of Career Assessment* 5 (1): 27–30.

Meir, E., A. Tziner, and Y. Glazner. 1997. "Environmental Congruence, Group Satisfaction, and Job Satisfaction." *Journal of Career Assessment* 5 (3): 84–91.

Mowday, R. 1978. "The Exercise of Upward Influence in Organizations." *Administrative Science Quarterly* 23: 137–156.

Myers, I., M. McCaulley, N. Quenk, and A. Hammer. 1998. *Myers-Briggs Type Indicator Manual,* 3rd ed. Palo Alto, CA: Consulting Psychologists Press, 171–222.

Perosa, L., and S. Perosa. 1997. "Assessments for Use with Mid-Career Changers." *Journal of Career Assessment* 5 (2): 58–61.

Sarbin, T. 1954. "Role Theory." In *Handbook of Social Psychology,* edited by G. Lindzey. Reading, MA: Addison-Wesley.

Schmidt, F., and J. Hunter. 1998. "The Validity and Utility of Selection Methods in Personnel Psychology: Practical and Theoretical Implications of 85 Years of Research Findings." *Psychological Bulletin* 124 (23): 262–274.

Shipper, F., and C. Wilson, 1991. "The Impact of Managerial Behaviors on Group Performance, Stress, and Commitment." Paper presented at The Research Conference on Leadership, Center for Creative Leadership, Colorado Springs, CO.

U.S. Department of Defense. 1984. *Manual for the Armed Services Vocational Aptitude Battery.* North Chicago, IL: U.S. Military Entrance Processing Command.

Critical Lessons in Talent Management

THE SEVEN CRITICAL lessons facing healthcare organizations in recruiting and retaining leadership talent, described fully in previous chapters, are key lessons to be learned. A summary of these lessons, wihth action steps organizations can take to meet each challenge, is provided below.

1. MAKE THE TALENT MANAGEMENT PROCESS A TOP STRATEGIC PRIORITY

As simple as it sounds, organizations that make this issue an absolute top strategic initiative will win the war for talent. They will excel in the years ahead, gaining talent and effectively meeting continued recruitment challenges.

Action step: Make talent management a top board initiative. Set specific goals and discuss them at each board and senior management meeting.

2. GAIN CONSENSUS BEFORE BEGINNING A SEARCH

The senior leaders of successful healthcare organizations reach consensus about the need for the search and the search process before beginning a search. They resist the natural reaction that often develops when a vacancy occurs to simply begin a search. These leaders take time to consider and reach consensus on whether the position is needed and if so, whether responsibilities should be changed, and the type of person needed to replace the departing executive. Once interviews begin, candidates sense no conflict within the organization on the position need or the type of person required.

Action step: Conduct a position assessment and analysis before starting the recruiting process.

3. DESIGNATE A SEARCH MANAGER

Healthcare organizations succeed in search efforts because they have a single person committed to managing the process from start to finish. Perhaps a human resources executive is assigned this task and given the full authority to manage all aspects of the search. Search steps are scheduled and proceed as scheduled, sending a positive signal to prospective candidates on the seriousness of the search effort.

Action step: Appoint a search process manager and give him or her complete authority to move the search process forward. Consider ways to allow search consultants, if used, to manage this process on behalf of the organization and its board.

4. DEFINE REQUIRED SKILLS, COMPETENCIES, CHARACTERISTICS, TRAITS

Successful healthcare organizations define the qualifications for the most preferred candidate in as much detail as possible. A description of specific skills, such as "has experience working with physicians during merger," or "has managed bond financings" appear in the place of ambiguous descriptions, such as "effective communication skills."

Action step: Draft specific qualifications statements for prospective leaders.

5. MAINTAIN FOCUS AND MOMENTUM

Healthcare organizations successful at recruiting high quality leadership talent keep their eye on the ball, maintaining focus and momentum throughout the talent recruitment and management process. Leaders regularly voice their continuing commitment to the process's high strategic priority.

Action step: Ensure that talent management receives continued top priority status, especially during times of leadership vacancies.

6. EFFECTIVELY INTEGRATE NEW MANAGERS AND EXECUTIVES

New leaders receive extensive and effective orientation within successful healthcare organizations. Their integration is planned and plans are implemented.

Action step: Evaluate and make formal the process used to orient and integrate new leaders.

7. PROVIDE FOR LEADERSHIP DEVELOPMENT

Healthcare organizations successful at recruiting and retaining high quality leadership talent make leadership development a top priority. They hire the best talent to lead the development effort and fund it appropriately. Leaders' continued growth ensures personal *and* organizational success.

Action step: Make leadership development a key organizational priority.

CONCLUDING COMMENTS

In closing, readers are reminded of the often-repeated statement that unfortunately has become a cliché, "People are our most important assets." Many organizations state this, but how few really practice it! Labor and leadership shortages make it vital for organizations to make the statement happen. Senior leadership must consider it daily, set and review aggressive goals and targets to address it, and make it a part of their organizational fabric. Healthcare organizations that accomplish these tasks will be the ones described in the best practices books of the later twenty-first century. They will make the difference in people's lives and in their communities. They will win the war for talent. After an almost thirty-year career focused on finding, placing, and developing talent, this author believes that identifying, recruiting, selecting, and developing executive healthcare talent has never been as important as it is now.

Good luck!

Index

Executive search firm, 11; contingency firms, 182–183; evaluation checklist, 192; expectations, 191–194; generalist, 184–185; need assessment, 185–188; process management, 44, 47; retained firms, 183–184; selection, 189–191; sourcing, 68; specialized, 184–185; use of, 181–182

Fernandez-Araoz, Claudio, 49
Flexible leadership, 27

Gadon, H., 121
General Electric, 27
Generalist firms, 184–185
Goal orientation, 30–31
Goleman, Daniel, 27
Governance Institute, 149
Group think, 98, 105
Gubman, Edward L., 18, 20–21, 30

Healthcare administration, 3
Healthcare Research and Development Institute, 2
Hiring decisions, 10; additional information needs, 100–101; background checks, 104; challenges, 97–99; consequences of, 7–8; criteria, 106–107; critical elements, 99–100; final evaluation, 106–107, 114–115; interview team input, 104–106; prior work experience, 102; reference checks, 103–104
Hiring process: advertising, 66–67; attributes, 50; bias, 98; candidate care, 87–89; candidate screening, 72–76; competencies, 50; employment contracts, 109–111, 116; executive search firms, 181–195; human resource staff, 67–68; Internet postings, 67; interview, 79–89; job function details, 47; management of, 44, 47; offer, 108–109; position need assessment, 41; position specification, 49–50; preparation stage, 39–51; psychological tests, 87; qualifications, 48; search committees, 161–173; search

firms, 44, 47, 68; search strategy, 41, 43–44; selective, 18; sourcing, 65–76; talent management and, 17–18; timetable, 44, 45–46, 51
Hogan, Joe, 6
Hogan, Joyce, 40
Hogan, Robert, 40
Holistic screening, 74
Hunt-Scanlon Corporation, 195
Hurdle screening, 74–75

Internal talent, 188
Internet postings, 67
Interview, 7, 10; assessment, 206; bias, 40; candidate care, 87–89; evaluation bias, 85–86; evaluation tools, 85, 92–93, 94–96; follow-up, 87; pre-screening, 80; process management, 86–87; purpose, 80–81; questions, 82, 84–85; search committee process, 170–171; team, 81–82; time allotment, 83; training, 82–83
Job description, 49, 176–177
Job functions, 53–54, 59–60
Johnson & Johnson, 24–26
Jones, Russ, 67
Josefowitz, N., 121

Katz, Michael, 22
Kennedy Information Inc., 195

Leadership: demographics, 2, 6–7; identification, 10; orientation periods, 8; positions, 2; retention, 4–5; senior-level turnover, 8–9; shortages, 1–3, 6–7, 8–9; styles, 27–28; teams, 8, 29–30
Leadership development, 4; approaches to, 145–146; curriculum, 154–155, 156–157; demographics, 6–7; expansion opportunities, 146–147; focus, 6; identification process, 142–143; performance measures, 148; prioritization, 19; program creation, 143–144; progression program, 152–153; promotion from within, 146; provisions, 219–220; resources, 147; senior executive participation in, 144; strategies,

About the Author

CARSON F. DYE, FACHE, is a management and search consultant with Witt/Kieffer Ford Hadelman and Lloyd who conducts chief executive officer, senior executive, and physician executive searches for a variety of healthcare organizations.

For thirty years, he has worked in various ways to find and develop effective leadership. His consulting experience includes strategic planning, organizational design, and physician leadership. He also assists boards in executive and physician compensation, conducts board retreats, and provides counsel in chief executive officers' employment contracts and evaluation matters. He is certified to work with the Hogan Assessment Systems tools for selection, development, and executive coaching.

Prior to entering executive search, Mr. Dye was a principal and director of Findley Davies, Inc.'s Health Care Industry Consulting Division. Prior to his consulting career, he served as chief human resources officer at St. Vincent Medical Center, Ohio State

University Medical Center, and Children's Hospital Medical Center.

Mr. Dye has been named as a physician leadership consultant expert on the LaRoche National Consultant Panel and is a member of the Governance Institute Governance One Hundred. He works with Dick Rand as a special advisor to The Healthcare Roundtable. He also serves on the faculty of the graduate program in management and health services policy at Ohio State University where he teaches both physician leadership and organizational behavior courses.

Since 1989, Mr. Dye has taught several programs for the American College of Healthcare Executives and frequently speaks for state and local hospital associations. He has also authored *Leadership in Healthcare: Values At the Top* (Health Administration Press 2000), the winner of the 2001 James A. Hamilton Book of the Year. In addition, he has authored *Executive Excellence: Protocols for Healthcare Leaders, Second Edition*, and *Protocols for Health Care Executive Behavior* (Health Administration Press 1993) and written several professional journal articles on leadership and human resources.

Mr. Dye has had a life-long interest in leadership and its impact upon organizations and has studied how values drive leadership and their effect on change management. He is also a student of groups and organizational structure and their impact upon strategy and organizational success.

Mr. Dye earned his BA from Marietta College and his MBA from Xavier University.